The Things My Best Friends Told Me
for the Camino and for Life

Kerry O'Regan

The Things My Best Friends Told Me for the Camino and for Life

The Things My Best Friends Told Me for the Camino and for Life
ISBN 978 1 74027 546 0
Copyright © text Kerry O'Regan 2009
Cover photo: a pilgrim sculpture on Alto del Perdon – hill of forgiveness
'The Journey', from *The House of Belonging* by David Whyte, used with permission from Many Rivers Press, Langley, Washington, USA – www.davidwhyte.com

First published 2009
Reprinted 2015

GINNINDERRA PRESS
PO Box 3461 Port Adelaide 5015
www.ginninderrapress.com.au

Sometimes it takes
a great sky
to find that

first, bright
and indescribable
wedge of freedom
in your own heart.

Sometimes with
the bones of the black
sticks left when the fire
has gone out

someone has written
something new
in the ashes of your life.
*You are not leaving
you are arriving.*

David Whyte – 'The Journey'

I didn't expect to discuss the Sapir-Whorf theory of linguistics with a German language teacher and an Iranian paediatrician while a Korean student looked on in some puzzlement. I didn't expect that a ukulele-playing Honolulu-German born-again Christian with a toothy grin would buy me a beer and try to save my soul. I didn't expect to be abandoned by an ambulance in an unknown town in the north of Spain. I didn't expect the countryside to be so beautiful or the pilgrim hostels, the albergues, to be on the whole so pleasant. But then, I didn't really know what to expect.

Some people, when they come to a 'who am I? what am I? what is life all about?' point in their lives buy a little red sports car. I decided to walk the Camino. Though 'decide' isn't quite the right word. It was stranger than that.

What I had decided to do was retire from full-time work on my sixty-third birthday. Someone asked, Are you going to travel when you retire?

No, I'm not much into travelling, but I am going to walk the Camino. Really? Did I say that? I knew practically nothing of it. Only vaguely knew of friends of friends who had done it and here I was making this absolute and unequivocal statement of intent. So of course, having said it out loud, I had to do it. An ageing, mild-mannered recently retired academic, ex-Catholic Quaker, only moderately fit and not at all into travel or long-distance walking. I was going to walk an ancient seven hundred and fifty kilometre pilgrimage across the top of Spain.

One of the things I did know was that a pilgrim carries a staff. So one day walking in the bush near Adelaide, I found myself a likely stick, took it home, cleaned it up, and invited my friends to a farewell party where they could write on it messages of encouragement. For those times when I felt lonely or discouraged. And a way of somehow carrying them all with me on my journey. Each day on the Camino I read those messages as I reflected on what that day had brought. And many times I would say to another pilgrim as they told me their story, Well, there's a message on my stick that says…

So here they are: the messages my friends wrote. They shaped the way I gave meaning to my experience, both of the Camino and of my other pilgrimage in the big wide world. And my responses to them, jottings from my journal, some fragments, some longer.

'As you set out for Ithaka...'

Having decided, I needed to prepare. What could I find out about this Camino business? Plenty of books. Except the ones by Paolo Coelho and Shirley MacLaine. I resisted those for reasons of personal prejudice. Just before I left, a friend found the MacLaine one on a throw-out table. It was as I expected, though it did contain one useful piece of advice which came in handy later. Plenty of websites too. Blogs by the score. I read somewhere it was the most blogged journey on the planet. Wonder why?

Where to go, where to stay, how and when to get there? The reading helped with those decisions. That was fun, though a travel agent even vaguely interested in the Camino would have been better.

What to take, what to wear? What not to? Usually an extra-light traveller, I relished pushing that to an extreme. I cut the covers and introductory waffle out of my guidebook and planned to shed the rest as I walked. Which I did. That was more than a practical benefit. Discarding the bits I no longer needed was strangely satisfying. And I ended the Camino with no guidebook at all.

I had been walking up to an hour a day plus a little yoga and weight work, but that was not nearly enough. I took on a more rigorous schedule building up to four-hour blocks of walking, and daily foot and leg exercises to prepare them for the long trek. The schedule included walking sections of the coastal path from the north to the south of Adelaide. I'd drive my car to the starting point, walk for two hours, then turn around and walk back to my car again. Of course, I needed to know the turn-back point so I could start from there next time.

One time I clambered up from the path to get my bearings. The houses were big and beautiful, the collection of cars in each multi-car garage worth more than my car and house put together. No street sign that I could see. A woman emerged from one of the houses. She obviously belonged. Dressed for walking, pack on my back, I obviously didn't.

I asked her about it. The location, that is. No welcoming smile. Just a slight raising of the perfectly-shaped eyebrows and a slight tightening around the perfectly-coloured mouth. There. Those large brass letters on the high stone wall. That was the street name, if street was good enough a word. Not the usual pole and label arrangement, but fair enough. Now I could find it again. She probably fumigated the place as soon as I left. Or at least had someone sweep it. I thanked her cheerily enough and headed off. And hugged a wicked little thought to myself: you don't know the worst of it – I just peed on your beach.

I didn't forget the spiritual side. If I was to be a pilgrim, I'd better prepare that way as well. After a Quaker retreat, I gathered together a little group of fellow pilgrims, not of the Camino but of life. I'd thought to call us Los Peregrinos, the pilgrims, but David, one of the group, said that sounded like a mariachi band. So I abandoned the idea. We were just us and we met each month for a year or so. We talked of our own journeys, what was happening for us, what sense we made of it, and what we did about it. Even better, I called in the big guns, so to speak. My sister Ann is a Catholic nun and this is, after all, her area of expertise. We live at opposite ends of the country, so it had to be in writing. Not a bad way to go. You mull over things and you probably try harder with the words. We puzzled over some things. Quakers and Catholics are very different. But our sisterly affection and mutual pig-headedness kept us hanging in.

***

And then there I was, finally in Spain. That first night, sitting alone in my hotel room wondering how it would all be. Even as the what-if demons danced about in my head, I knew that that's where they were. Not on the road in front of me or anywhere outside myself. They were all within. Challenges there would be in the weeks ahead, but any monsters would be of my own creating.

'Left foot forward, right foot forward; repeat...'

For most of our life, once we get the hang of it, walking's an automatic thing. We're hardly conscious of it. But the first day on the Camino was not like that. The path, steep slopes of thick mud. Wet and slippery. Where best to put each foot so it didn't sink into the mud. How not to slide and slither bodily into it. How to lift my foot and not leave my shoe behind. At each lift, my foot was coated with more and more of the sticky stuff. Thicker and heavier.

By the end of the day, the mud was gone but it was still steep and it was stony. Now a deep layer of small, loose stones. I was tired. To keep going, I willed each step. I would have just stopped if I hadn't said to each foot in turn, Now you go, now you. But I did it. All the way to that day's goal of Zubiri. Muddy and sore, but no real harm done. I had walked the first day of my Camino.

That conscious walking became part of my Camino. Every step a decision about where to put my foot so that I wouldn't: 1: sink into the mud; 2: slip over; 3: twist my ankle; 4: fall headlong; 5: cause a minor rock fall. Until one moment I lost that concentration and had one of my biggest adventures of the Camino. But that was still some weeks off.

At that time of year in Spain it was bright daylight until around ten at night. So when at Cadzadilla I looked out the upper window of the albergue, I could see him clearly: the barefoot peregrino. He was even scruffier than most, with shabby clothes and long unkempt hair. And he walked slowly, placing each foot carefully and deliberately in front of the other, seeking the sparse patches of grass where he could. The path had been rough, as it was most days. But this day it was hardened clay studded with stones, many of them large ones. I had picked my steps carefully, avoiding the worst, but even so, my feet complained all the way. How would it be with no shoes? It was painful just to watch him.

Someone said they'd passed him earlier. And here he was, arriving, some eight hours after they had. Perhaps he was practising a slow, focused meditation, quite unlike my brisk haphazard effort. Or maybe it was a penitential act of some kind. I'll probably never know.

'Enjoy a road less travelled'

Walking the Camino is an odd thing to do. I knew that. So did the couple beside me on the flight to Athens. They were off to cruise for two weeks around the Greek islands while I was heading for five or so weeks of arduous walking. I was odd.

Another stop, Singapore, was a great place to shop, but the glitzy stores at Changi airport quite disturbed me. There's something about the bright lights and the glitter. The frenzied buying and selling of more and more stuff.

Yet the shops in the old cobbled streets of Pamplona quite enchanted me. There, buying and selling wasn't the focus. The locals seemed out to enjoy themselves and each other. They gathered on the streets to talk and laugh together and the rows of shops provided the picturesque backdrop. Consumerism seems okay in a pretty setting.

My reluctance to shop was recorded. I'm now an official statistic. At Rome airport I met a market researcher for the Italian tourist industry. Just as well, for them, that not all transit passengers are like me. I had to confess that in the two hours I spent amid those glamorous airport shops, my sole purchase was one bottle of water.

***

The albergue at Burgos was set in open parkland at the far end of the city. Green grass, shady trees, family groups picnicking or playing with balls, kids, and dogs. Or just strolling through the park on the warm summer night. The albergue was large, hot and crowded. A brown wooden building crammed with double bunks and nothing else. No kitchen and no place to get food. One of the hospitaleros said you could get cheap meals at the university just over the road a bit.

I found what I hoped was the campus. Serious-looking buildings with a few young people, probably students, straggling outside. Then one building with a few more people and a few more lights. It seemed the right one. I lined up with the dozen or so students and placed my tray on the cafeteria-style counter along with the others. There's no way that I, a white-haired Australian, could be mistaken for a Spanish university student, but no one pointed or stared or showed any surprise at my unlikely presence.

I wanted to say that I wasn't trying to pass myself off as a student and get a free meal. So when it came to my turn I pointed at my tray and asked, 'Peudo…? Peregrina? (Can I…? A pilgrim?)' The serving woman filled my tray so it must have been okay. It was a big empty place, like any student caf after hours. I sat at one of the tables and tried to be inconspicuous; and ate my meal without anyone calling the police or demanding that I leave.

I don't know what the other ninety or so albergue residents did that night, but I had a perfectly adequate feed for around three euros. Even then I had to go chasing someone to pay for it.

***

My big adventure involved a detour to Melgar de Fernamental. It was a town well off the Camino where I had an emergency patch-up of a cut forehead. It was a drab little place and I felt very lost there. I was very lost there. No arrows, no shells, no pilgrims, no Camino.

The Camino had become a familiar place, a comfortable place. With all our diversity, and our odd looks, we fitted somehow. People greeted us and wished us buen Camino. Conversation didn't stop, all eyes on us, as we entered a room, which was how I felt in Melgar de Fernamental. After two weeks of walking, I'd gained a sense of belonging. I was part of this ant-like procession of pilgrims who had a job to do and a place to go. And that's what we were doing.

***

The municipal albergue in Santa Catalina was down a tiny laneway, much less travelled than it used to be. Two bright shiny new albergues, privately owned and on the main road, had seen to that. But my guidebook told of this old one, tucked away out of sight and now mostly ignored by the passing peregrinos.

I chose the municipal one on principle. Official support of pilgrims was a good thing and I wanted to encourage that. So I headed down the narrow pathway between two buildings. The poor old place looked neglected. There were cracks in the walls and everything about it was old and tired. The door was open but there was no one around. A hand-written sign said it would be open at two, but was that to be taken seriously? I went off to find some lunch. Still no one, so I stretched out on the grass for an hour or so's rest.

In the end I let myself in. What I found was pretty basic. The shower roses had gone, so having a shower was like standing under a running tap. Hot water, though. But no toilet paper. Everything a bit bleak-looking.

It was hot and I was tired so, feeling rather like Goldilocks, I selected the bed that looked most 'just right' and went to sleep, expecting the bears to return from their walk at any moment. No bears and no hospitalero either, by the time I awoke at around six.

A young Spanish man and, later, an Irish man arrived. Just the three of us. Then, finally, a local turned up bearing two rolls of toilet paper and asking for three euros from each of us. And left us to it. Plenty of space there. Though the mattress sagged and my torch, which started the night under my pillow, ended up under my hip. Still, there's worse things than sleeping in a hammock – especially in a nearly-empty room. That was a luxury.

I don't expect that albergue will be there much longer. Shame really.

***

To walk slowly across a country is to see the fine grain of it, every stone, every blade of grass you pass. And to walk through the life of ordinary people. Occasionally, the path passed through tourist spots. Those places felt less authentic somehow. Though perhaps I was just getting sanctimonious about it. Tourists had as much right there as we did and probably did more for the local economy.

O'Cebeiro was a tourist destination as well as a popular stopping place on the Camino. You could tell by the tourist buses and the souvenir shops. It felt odd to have a different kind of stranger in town, besides us pilgrims. These others wore smart clothes and carried cameras. They strolled around, looking and buying and talking together. Without the purposeful stride of the walking peregrino or careful hobble of the one who had stopped for the night. I'm not sure if we were an irritation to them or one of the sights to be seen.

The people of northern Spain were mostly poor, and I felt the privilege of walking right through their lives. The shepherds with their flock of a hundred sheep. The cowherds coaxing their ten cows down the road to wherever it was they were meant to go. The bread van beeping its way through the village streets. The field workers, the women in their bandanas and drab shapeless smocks. Men and women digging the earth with garden hoes, cutting back growth with reaping hooks. Buildings of old, old, stone, old as the hills themselves. All very romantic, but no doubt hard work. Really hard work.

Many of these folk lifted their heads to greet the passing stream of peregrinos and wish us well. A few asked me where I was from. At least, I think that's what they were asking. Their response was always the same – a laugh of delight and 'Australia! Ah, kangaroos!' – and we'd laugh together.

Such hard labour, with few machines to help. There'd been a wedding in Portomarin and the plaza around the church was littered with rice and fragments of coloured paper – a great swirling sea of it. I watched a man with just a broom and dustpan spend an hour or so sweeping it clean. Or trying to. It was a battle the wind was destined to win. But that was not good enough. Stern words from the supervisor and the sweeper was back to spend more time, more effort, on his hopeless task. I'd had enough by this stage and went off and left him to it. It was discouraging enough just to watch.

'Step by step the longest march shall be won'

The first two weeks were through open country. The path with its guiding yellow arrows. That was a constant. Beyond that, neat fields of crops in chequered arrays. Hills and mountains with their thick leafy forests. Villages every little while. And, after drought-ridden Australia, water that seemed to flow through everything. Extravagantly. Rivers and streams and the constantly-running fountains. Even the forests dripped with moisture. I thought it might be like that all the way.

But then came the shock of Burgos. There was supposed to be another way into the city, but I couldn't find that. I followed the arrows and they followed the busy main road. The noise of the traffic was bad enough. And the way it moved. Rapid and random. Stopping and starting, speeding and slowing, revving and braking. Trucks and cars and buses and people. So many people. Traffic lights and traffic fumes. And other city smells. And mile after mile of industry. Hot. And dry. It was a shock.

Some pilgrims bussed in, but I walked it. I thought about the bus, but decided no. Not from a sense of righteousness or of penitence. This was the Camino too, just as much as the green and pleasant land had been. No one said it would beautiful all the way. There were times when it was a tough slog and you just did it. Like life really.

Bron bussed in. But next morning she felt so bad she caught the bus out again and walked in this time. At least I didn't do that.

***

Once I'd passed the halfway point, I felt I'd begun my descent of the Camino mountain. It's hard to know just where the halfway point is. The distance from Roncesvalles to Santiago is somewhere between seven hundred and forty and eight hundred kilometres, depending on which guidebook or signpost you believe.

I met a young German man who had a pedometer attached to his foot. He'll know exactly how far. If he only recorded when he walked in a forward direction. Which he probably did. He was that kind of German.

***

Some nights I'd think, okay, I've done it now; I'm ready to stop. Tomorrow will just be more of the same: wake up, have breakfast, walk, stop, wash myself, wash my clothes, write, potter around, eat, sleep. And so will the day after that, and the day after that.

But then tomorrow came and, while it was all of that, it was also different and wonderful – and challenging – in that day's way. And not quite like any other day.

'Make every post a winner'

There was a clear hierarchy among the pilgrims. Some ways of travelling were definitely more worthy than others. The real winners were those who had come from afar, Holland or Germany. The ones who walked out of their front door and just keep walking until they got to Santiago. Or, better still, Finisterre. Or, better still, those who got there, then turned round and walked all the way back again. Although this last was perhaps too extreme.

Those at the bottom of the pilgrim stakes were the ones who walked the bare one hundred kilometres that would earn them the pilgrim certificate, the compostela. Especially those who stayed in pre-booked hotels. Those who were transported to and from those hotels by car and carried nothing more than water and the odd gourmet snack. Those at the real bottom of the pile even had a van which brought the gourmet snacks to them at pre-arranged spots along the way.

Some of the real pilgrims were scathing of these losers. It was a fake compostela they received. When they arrived at heaven, God would turn them away. It wasn't His compostela they bore in their hands but a travel agent's.

I'm sure you could find chapter and verse to support the losers. I'm thinking of the workers in the vineyard. The ones who arrived right at the end of the harvest and received the same payment as those who'd laboured the whole time. Always seemed a bit unfair to me, but that's what it says.

If there is a Big Accountant in the sky, though that's not part of my cosmology, I suspect the system of reckoning will not be one that we'd ordain.

***

The daily 'post' was arriving at that day's destination, each albergue a marker of progress along the way. Each stop had its own character and each marked an important achievement. I could have given myself a hard time, in that twenty kilometres a day wasn't far. Not compared with what others did. But mostly I didn't give myself a hard time. I celebrated each of those twenty kilometres as a little win. Appreciated the time it allowed to pause along the way, to sit in a still place, to linger over coffee, to wander around a village.

And when I arrived in at an albergue, I usually got the pick of the beds. And a hot shower, and time to wash and dry my clothes. And time to sit and write. All wins, that's for sure.

***

At Sahagun I met a Belgian man who had cycled two hundred kilometres that day. He'd started his Camino from his home in Antwerp and was expecting to maintain that pace to Santiago. Every day he rode flat out for eleven hours. Arriving in the quickest possible time was what it was about. He wins my prize for that little contest.

He couldn't imagine why anyone would go at any other pace. Other than the fastest they possibly could. It was nice to see him and the barefoot pilgrim on the same day. Both winners in their own terms.

***

I lost my stick. On my second last day of walking it disappeared. At first it felt like a major loss. I had planned to take it to Finisterre and throw it dramatically into the sea and now that wasn't possible.

I had stayed the night at a tiny albergue at Boente and left my precious stick leaning against the wall beside the front door. I thought I'd pick it up in the morning. There were some Germans staying there who noticed and commented on it. Not to me, to each other, but I thought nothing much of that. It wasn't in itself an attractive object. A crooked bit of stick, rather the worse for five weeks wear and weather, its hand-written messages half worn off.

But when I left at around seven in the morning, my stick was nowhere to be seen. Maybe the hospitaleros had taken it inside when they were locking up. But they were not yet up and, except for the exit door, the place was locked. Or maybe the Germans, or someone else, had seen it there still and thought to find the owner. Or maybe it was there, right in front of me, and I just couldn't see it. Whatever the story, it was not to be found.

Sometimes I find it hard to let go. Of things, of people, of ideas, of situations. And I know that it's important. To be able to do that. To cherish the thing, person, idea, situation, while it is there. But to let it go, graciously and gratefully, when that time comes. Which may not be the time I'd choose.

Perhaps my stick is having another life, a richer one than being tossed into the sea. Perhaps the messages, those that remain, are inspiring, encouraging, or at least intriguing someone else. Leading them to wonder about its story and to ask questions.

I was sorry my stick-throwing plans had been aborted. But I came to accept it. There's a middle way somewhere between controlling all the events of our lives and being totally passive. Loosening my grasp on my stick, the day before Santiago, fits with that way.

'Happy wandering'

I passed a drinking fountain along the way. I passed many drinking fountains along the way, but this one was special. It was part of a miracle story. There were quite a few miracle stories along the Camino too. But more fountains. Lots more. At least that I knew of.

Here, in medieval times, a pilgrim arrived overcome with thirst. A second pilgrim turned up and offered the first some water. Two problems. The deal was he had to renounce God to get the water. Secondly, the water-bearer wasn't a pilgrim at all. It was the devil in pilgrim disguise.

The first pilgrim said no deal. So then St James himself arrived on the scene. He led the real pilgrim, the thirsty one, to the life-giving spring. Even provided a scallop shell to drink with. And the fountain is still there on the very spot of the miracle. It's provided water to pilgrims ever since, without them having to pass the test first.

Except, so my guidebook said, it's been prone to drying up in recent times. A sign, it said, of the modern doubts about God. Maybe.

***

Castrojeriz was a good place to spend a day. Not that I actually chose it. I fell and cut my head so decided not to walk the next day. I was at Castrojeriz so that's where I stayed.

It was bigger than a village, more like a small town. Most villages had their shops scattered randomly, tucked away in little corners. Castrojeriz had a main street of them, all lined up in order. There was even a money machine. I was running low on cash but anxious about trusting my card to a strange machine. What if it ate it? What if it said I had no money? I'd heard stories, but it was either that or run out of money. With a great leap of faith, I slid my card into the slot and waited. Miracle. A multilingual machine. We negotiated the release of a handful of notes. It wouldn't let on how much I had left, but as long as it and its fellows kept handing over, I didn't need to know. Or so I told myself.

Best of all, high on the hill above the town were the ruins of an old castle. I wasn't going anywhere else, so I ventured up. The way was steep and I was alone. Except for a couple of shepherds. They sat by the path with their dogs and their small flock of sheep, and their mobile phone. I had all day so I didn't need to hurry.

As a child, I read schoolgirl adventure books. I'd get them from the library on Friday and read in bed, late into the night, until my eyes refused to keep going. There was usually some kind of mysterious goings-on at the ruins of the old abbey or castle. And I felt deprived. Australia provided no such ruins, but Castrojeriz castle offered more than enough. Crumbling, but still substantial, walls, narrow stone stairs, arches and openings of all descriptions. And places to sit among the rambling wildflowers. Old fantasies could run riot.

I was ten years old. Plucky little Hilary and bookish, bespectacled Millicent, were playing sleuth to the nefarious doings of the mean prefect, Enid, and her no-good uncle. Strange lights in the castle ruins. They saved the day. And the school from imminent closure, or the parish silver from being stolen, or Enid from a life of crime. Or something.

Ah. Deprived no more. A forever itch finally scratched. And by a castle in Spain.

Back to Spain and to the Camino. The view as from the top of the world. Fields and villages for ever all around. Thin lines of brown roads crossing through them. And there, from Castrojeriz, the path leading up and up and up some more, to the high flatness of the meseta. Manana's journey.

***

I've been something of a wanderer. Not a walking kind of wanderer, but with another kind of restlessness. I've not lived long in one place. I've moved on. Different house, different city, different state. But I might be cured of that. Being on the Camino was being constantly on the move. Each night in a different place, talking with different people, sleeping in a different bed. I yearned to just stop and stay. To be still.

'Travel in peace'

I think I was born a pacifist. Perhaps there's a gene for it. I certainly don't remember a time when I wasn't. Not really. Peace is an alluring ideal. But how do we get it? There are Quaker committees for peace and justice. But how can you have both? People fight for justice. There must be a way that doesn't involve fisticuffs down behind the shed. Or the international equivalent.

I spent my first day in Pamplona, the place where they do the running of the bulls. But that wasn't till next month. Fortunately. Instead, that night a group of grim-faced humans paraded through the streets. They walked silently and each carried a banner with a black and white photograph. This was not a fun gathering. It was sombre. But what was it all about?

The hotel man said the photographs were of Basque separatists detained for their activities. Terrorists or heroes, depending on your point of view. The marchers opposed their detention.

And later a choir singing in the street, what could only be songs of protest. With suitable passion. Much red and black, the men wearing those flat black berets, red or black scarves around their necks. I don't know where justice sits in it all. Or peace.

***

Mostly I walked alone. That way I found my own Kerry peace. The peace that you have to burrow right down inside to discover. The rhythm of walking helped. And the stick. Sometimes it was all I could hear. I counted my steps. 1, 2, 3, 4…1, 2, 3, 4…with the tap of my stick after each 1. And breathed to that rhythm. In-tap, 2, 3, 4. Out-tap, 2, 3, 4. It's stilling. To walk that way for thirty-seven days is to know peace.

That was sometimes at odds with the history of the place. A short way out from Ventosa was an odd-looking hut by the side of the road. Roughly beehive-shaped, made of stone and fairly new. I stopped for a snack in its shelter and wondered about it. There on the other side was a notice explaining. Not the shape, that's still mysterious. The hut, it said, commemorates the defeat by Roldan, the Christian warrior, of the Muslim giant, Ferragut. It's something of a David and Goliath tale and, depending on the version, the fatal wound was inflicted by a David-type stone or by a knife stab to the navel. Whatever the means, the giant was slain and victory won for Charlemagne and, ultimately, for Christian Spain. Not a place of peace.

***

Between Pamplona and Zariquiegui was the site where Charlemagne's troops defeated the Muslim army. Still that conflict goes on, in other places in other ways.

And the poppy fields. Each time a reminder of slaughters where the red was not only from the poppies.

***

In the early days, people used to do it a lot. Die on the Camino. They still do it now, though not so many. And we don't need special cemeteries and such to cope with it. There were monuments along the way. Mostly at the beginning and at the end. Walkers with heart attacks. Cyclists knocked off their bikes. I could understand the beginning ones. The heart saying, Hey, you didn't prepare me for this. The cyclist's inattention to the unfamiliar traffic. I was surprised, though, by the end ones. It seemed a shame to come so far and then die within a day's walk of reaching your goal. Maybe the body gets confused. Okay, that's it, I've done what I had to do and stops. Dead.

But they did make me think. The limited span of life's journey. For me, and I suspect for others, there was a sense of that before I set off. I wrote a new will and put my affairs in order. There seemed a chance that my life's journey, and not just the journey of my life, would be completed on the Camino. But it wasn't.

***

After leaving Lorca I passed fields of poppies. Dots of red spattered across the green. And felt sad at the sight. It reminded me of the poppy fields of Flanders and the young men who died in those fields. And in all the other places in all the other wars.

I've always resisted the poppy sellers on Armistice Day. I don't know how to deal with that stuff. It seems to say what a great and glorious thing it was, these young men dying for their country. I see war as a tragic and futile mistake and I don't want to celebrate it.

I picked one of the poppies, growing there in Spain, and wore it. My own little ritual where there was no one to mistake my meaning. Not that I really knew my meaning. Except to express my sorrow for all those who killed and all those who were killed in war. My sorrow for their courage. And for their fear. My sorrow for those who knew and loved them. And for those who would have known and loved them, if they'd lived longer. I don't know if I'll wear a poppy next Armistice Day, but I wore one that day.

'Step lightly, with spin'

Each albergue had a different quality to it and sometimes that was challenging. The first night at Roncesvalles was like being in an old-fashioned boarding school. We had to take off our boots and place them in racks by the door. Some folk had trudged through mud up the Pyrenees, but some of us were fresh off the bus, boots pristine. But no; one rule for all.

Then we were ushered into the biggest dormitory you could imagine. Seventy double bunks jammed together in pairs. Quite an introduction to communal sleeping. Like sharing a double bed with a total stranger while all around you others were doing the same. We were allocated our bed by number as we arrived, and no arguing about that either. Lights out at ten and on again at six. Everybody up. All this overseen by a pleasant enough, but certainly no-nonsense, group of housemasters.

The next day I arrived at Zubiri around lunch time. The cheaper municipal albergue wasn't opening till four, so I stayed at a small, private establishment. My body was aching for a shower and a bed. It was worth the extra euros. But it felt clinical and commercial. The woman took our names and stamped our credential with a remote efficiency. There was no sense of connection.

But really, it was just a matter of spin. The housemasters at Roncesvalles keep the place in good order. The woman at Zubiri provides a service, runs a business, and there's nothing wrong with that.

***

There's something freeing about travelling lightly. One change of clothes, one small guidebook which I discarded page by page as I went.

Harvey was an Englishman now living in Canada. He was big and looked strong, but had terrible trouble with his pack. It fitted badly and weighed him down. And hurt his shoulders. Maybe he could carry less, but no, he needed the essentials. What are the essentials? What a burden they can become.

I walked into the bathroom one morning, to go to the toilet and brush my teeth. The essentials. A woman was standing in front of the mirror, her toiletry essentials spread out in front of her. They fitted into a roll-up pouch made of fabric. Not just one pouch, but many little pockets, side by side. Each little pocket held a bottle or jar or tube filled with the products she needed to keep herself beautiful.

I had my toddler toothbrush. It was smaller than most. And sample-size toothpaste from the dentist. Soap. The one cake for everything, hair, body, clothes. And deodorant. That was essential. I didn't want to smell. But that was it. If I couldn't be beautiful with that lot, I wouldn't be beautiful.

I'd bought a new camera for the trip. Duty-free, so I had to bring the sealed package with me through customs. Once past the barrier I could throw away the packaging, but what to do with rest, the accessories, the CD and the manual in four languages? I carried them with me on the Camino but, in my mind at least, they grew heavier and heavier and became more and more bothersome, the further I went. I wanted to be rid of them, but post offices in Spain are hidden away. The few that exist. Perhaps Spanish people don't write letters. Australian people probably don't write letters either but we still have post offices. The tiniest dot on a map, if it has nothing else, will have a post office. Probably a pub, but certainly a post office.

I found one eventually, one that was open, so sent off my unwanted camera stuff. I felt so lightened, much more than their size and weight would merit. It felt pure and clean to walk uncluttered. Uncluttered by stuff to carry and worry about, and uncluttered in my head. Stripped right, right back. Nothing to fuss with or be distracted by. Just me and my stick in the lightness of being.

***

The one thing I found most difficult to take lightly was the total lack of privacy. Some things we prefer do in private. Except when you were inside a toilet with a catch that worked, everything you did was on display for whoever was around at the time. How and when you slept, the movements and noises that accompanied that; what, when and how you ate; and how and when you attended to your personal hygiene. Shaving your face or your legs, plucking your eyebrows, cutting your toenails, flossing your teeth, dressing and undressing, were all carried out in company.

My heaving gut at Tarbedelos had me rushing to the toilet several times in the night. Noises magnify in the still night hours. Doors clicking, floors squeaking, toilets flushing. And those embarrassing noises we don't usually share. My gut-searing farts when I was ill, reverberating in the toilet bowl, sounding like a trumpet being blown apart.

We normally hide such things behind polite facades. But there were none. Sometimes not even physical barriers. Most shower cubicles had lockable doors. Perhaps shower curtains as well, though sometimes the bathrooms were unisex. But some had no protection at all.

At O'Cerbeiro the tiny shower cubicles were completely open. Not only that, the bathroom had huge picture windows. Through them we could see the magnificent vista of mountain ranges. But, more immediately, we could also see the grassy terrace just outside. And the pilgrims strolling past. Hi, guys, yes, this is us in our bathroom, showering, towelling, dressing.

Forget pretensions or affectations. Or even dignity. The most intimate parts of life were there on display. For all of us. And that was just the way it was.

***

The albergue at Cacabelos was like a prison complex. Not that I've been in one to know. A near-circle of orange-yellow cells abutted the church at either end and surrounded a central exercise yard. It wasn't really an exercise yard. More a place to wash and dry your clothes. And to sit in if the weather was kind. There was no other common space.

Unless you counted the toilet block. Each cell contained two beds, one either side of the door, with just the door-width space between. No windows. Too bad if you suffered from claustrophobia. And the whole place was locked down at eleven. But it was cheap, it was clean, and sleeping in a confined space with just one total stranger made a change from sleeping in a whole roomful of them.

'The end where we start from, we arrive to see the place for the first time'

Tardajos was a little village much like the hundreds of other little villages I walked through on the Camino. The streets were paved, narrow and sharply angled, more people-friendly than car-friendly. The houses joined one to the other and rising straight up from the streets with little or nothing in the way of footpaths. Nowhere much to be except inside the houses or on the streets. And it was there on the street in Tardajos that I saw something that took me back to my childhood.

I almost walked right over it. The faintly drawn outline of a hopscotch game. I recognised it because it was exactly the same as the ones I used to draw in the ground with a stick when I was a kid at school in Australia. And that was fifty-something years ago. It felt eerie. There is a way of doing hopscotch, a knowing, that transcends time, place and culture. How does that work? The kids here in Spain in the beginning of the twenty-first century using the very same pattern that I used in Australia all those years ago. Connected through hopscotch.

***

There was an odd collection of 'stuff' at many of the albergues. Chess sets and board games and a motley set of books in different languages, probably left by pilgrims seeking to lighten their load. At one albergue I found a cheap paperback copy of *Black Beauty*. That was a childhood favourite of mine and if I close my eyes I can see the book we had at home. Red-bound cover with slightly worn edges. Thick pages. We didn't have many books and I read it over and over.

This cheap little edition had a note about the author, Anna Sewell. It said she was a Quaker. I didn't know that. Her reverence for life extended to animals. She cared about how they were treated, or in her experience, mistreated. And she wanted to do something about that, which is why she wrote *Black Beauty*. The things you learn on the Camino. Not the things you expect.

***

When there isn't the busy clutter of everyday life to fill your head, there's space for other things to emerge. And for me these were sometimes memories from childhood.

I met a nurse, Liz. She changed the dressing on my cut forehead and told me she came from Shorncliff. Apparently it's now a beach suburb of Brisbane. Shorncliff. The word brought back so much. When I was a kid in Newmarket we used to have our school picnic at Shorncliff. Every year. We'd pack up our picnic gear and walk, in great excitement, to the train station. Not too many families had cars and, even if they did, the mums didn't drive them. We'd pile into the carriages with the long padded seats that went all the way across, put the windows and shutters up and down – the big heavy sort that dropped down into the wall cavity - and stick our heads out the windows until we got bits of soot in our eyes that our mothers got out with the corner of a hanky.

Even the nuns were cheerful on picnic day. No scowls, no scoldings and not a cane in sight. We'd leave our belongings and our mothers under the big shady trees and head straight for the water. Much splashing and squealing and a few sea lice and then lunch. Sandwiches and cordial while the mothers drank tea made with boiling water from the kiosk. And a slice of the watermelon some of the big boys had carried from the train.

Then a walk along the pier with maybe a penny or two for an arcade game. My favourite had a car steering wheel and a road that rolled toward you in an unpredictable way while you tried to keep the car on track. I fancy there was also a What the Butler Saw, but we didn't bother with that. Either we thought it too sinful or that pictures of a lady in limited stages of undress were not worth spending a penny on. Not that you'd see much in Queensland in the fifties. Besides, we'd seen our mothers in less.

The nuns went off and ate somewhere else. For some reason they weren't allowed to eat with others, which added to their mystique. Perhaps there was something odd about the way they did it or maybe they couldn't show their bodies functioning like ordinary human beings.

Time for a scramble round the cliffs and then take our sunburn home to show off the next day. No slip, slop, slap in those days.

All that from 'Shorncliff'. Liz said it's all been 'developed' now. I don't expect they have school picnics there any more.

***'

Many pilgrims come back to the Camino again and again. One Canadian couple were walking it for the third time. They said they liked walking, but it must be more than that. There were, after all, plenty of places to walk closer to home.

There were stories told and retold among the pilgrims. Stories of those who'd walked the Camino a dozen or more times and those who just kept doing it, backwards and forwards. The Canadians were surprised when I said this was my one and only. Whatever the Camino returns me to, I doubt it will be going back to the Camino.

***

After five weeks of walking, it began to feel like the ending, the last little bit of the Camino. I reckoned on five more days and started to feel the excitement of ending. But then, in Sarria, I had dinner with a young French woman who was just starting her Camino. We sat and talked and exchanged excitements. Her first day, one of my last. My ending, her beginning; both at the same spot. There, that time, that place, was not, in itself, a beginning or an ending. For us it was both. Endings and beginnings are not absolute: they're just us putting labels on things to make sense of them.

***

The last bit of the Camino was through shaded forest. I walked along, aware of nothing in particular, when suddenly I was noticing something. The leaves on the path. Why was I noticing them? Of course, they were gum leaves. And the smell. There among the Spanish trees were tall straight eucalypts, contributing more than their share of forest litter.

I felt no great pang of homesickness. Just a sense of comfort that those familiar trees were there with me on the Camino. I know nothing of the environmental issues. But it was like discovering that someone had remembered, after all, to pack your favourite old teddy bear.

***

Then finally Santiago. It was like living the last chapter of a cheap novel, where all the loose ends are hastily tidied up in a series of unlikely encounters.

Santiago is not a small place; four large squares, one on each side of the cathedral, and a confusing network of streets and shops. There was a low probability that you and any other particular person would be in the same place at the same time.

But first there was Liam, the Irish man who'd walked with me over the mountain when I felt so sick. Yes, thanks Liam, I'm fine now and, as you can see, have arrived safely in Santiago.

And the Swiss man from the albergue the previous night. His tendonitis had been so bad he could barely hobble from the dining table. He'd been a forty-plus kilometre a day man, but had taken all of that last day to walk, carefully and painfully, the last twenty kilometres into Santiago. And there he was.

And Sue, the young South African widow, who I had left in such a distressed state way back in Burgos. Here she was too, looking fit and healthy and with a gorgeous and attentive Italian in tow.

And the neatest little tying-off of all. I was having one final browse in a Santiago gift shop when someone called my name. It was Hannah, the first pilgrim I had spoken to on my first day. She had slept in the bunk below me that night in Roncesvalles. And here she was in Santiago the same time I was, the last pilgrim I would speak to on my last day. My alpha and omega pilgrim friend.

But, corny though that was, it wasn't quite the end. There was a postscript. After Santiago I went on to Finisterre. The end of the earth. And found an English man I had met some weeks before. Then he was travelling with a French woman. Now he was travelling with his wife. She had come to walk with him for the last little bit. I resisted the mischievous urge to ask about his earlier companion, in response, perhaps, to his likely fervent prayer. Though I'm sure he knew I was thinking the question. Of course the other woman may have been his cousin or an old family friend or just someone he was walking with for a while.

And then we all lived happily ever after. The End.

But even that wasn't quite the end. There was one final punchline. From a German pilgrim who looked a little rueful as he collected his compostela. We're not pilgrims any more, we're just tourists. And so it was. Or was it?

***

One of the outside walls of the Santiago cathedral has the first and last letters of the Greek alphabet carved into it. The alpha and the omega. Funny thing is, they're the wrong way round. Whether by accident or design, the omega comes before the alpha.

But then, endings and beginnings are curious things. Am I no longer a pilgrim? What does being a pilgrim mean? Beginnings, endings, leavings, arrivings are all jumbled together in a constantly changing kaleidoscope. We see new patterns, but we see the old ones as well. Familiar yet strange. We see them as if for the first time.

'Remember Conflict'

Quakers are good people and all-in-all a peaceable lot. Our Peace Testimony defines us and we try to live it. But we're still just human with the quirks and foibles that go with that. It's hard, the tension of being rugged individualists who also value peace and harmony. We're so committed to peaceful ways that we're not good with our own conflicts. We don't know how to do them. There's a saying that Quakers have lumpy carpets. So much keeps getting swept under.

It was like that before I left for the Camino. A time of conflict in our meeting and I was in the middle of it. More and more out of control, as time went on. Friends told me to not think about the problem, to put it aside, while I was on my pilgrimage.

I didn't not think about it. Neither did I wrestle with it. It just sat there in the background. Part of the fading wallpaper of my life. My distress fading with it. Washed away by those cleansing showers perhaps or stilled by the walking. It just didn't matter so much.

What I saw ahead of me was the last third (at most) of my life. I wanted that to be a joyous time. With some people, in some situations, I'm littler, meaner. I didn't want that. I wanted to be big and generous and joyous. And not just a layer of frosting on the top of life. I wanted it to go right through to the centre. Or come right out from the centre, more like. I didn't want to cause pain to others nor lay myself open to pain. Not if I could help it. Inner turmoil and anguish can be so destructive. And so littling. I saw that.

I wanted to be a Quaker, but I didn't want to rush back into the fray. If I could find a space in the meeting where I could be the person I wanted to be, that would be good. Otherwise, I might look elsewhere. Perhaps that's cowardly, but if so, then it's a coward, a calm one, that I chose to be.

'Wonder Woman...Go!'

I didn't feel like Wonder Woman most of the time. Twenty kilometres a day was a modest pace. Though I didn't suffer the blisters and tendonitis and inflammations that others did.

My biggest problem was my heels. After walking several hours, the soles of my feet, especially my heels, felt as though someone had been hammering them with little metal mallets. Which was, effectively, what I was doing to them.

When I was in training before I left Australia, my friend Deb gave me a box of 'lectric soda and a packet of glass marbles. You put the marbles in a footbath add water and the soda and rub your feet over the marbles. It's a great massage. As I walked I would fantasise about that. Imagine myself sitting with my feet in that nice warm tub, rubbing them on the marbles. Even the fantasy soothed my aching feet.

And I remembered what Shirley MacLaine had said. I can't recall which bit of her was hurting, but she remembered the Sherpas who walked effortlessly on the balls of their feet. Worth a try. I think it helped.

***

At Burgos I had my one and only cold shower. My pattern was to walk in the relative cool of the morning and arrive at the day's albergue nice and early. Mostly that meant before the showers had run cold. But it was a long, dreary walk through Burgos and doing the tourist bit in the cathedral took time. So it was late before I arrived at the albergue right on the other side of town. It was, however, one of the hottest days so I didn't really need to be a superhero to face the cold shower.

***

I still haven't really learned that I'm not Wonder Woman.

After I left the mountain retreat of Manjarin, I started to feel unwell. My gut was cramping. It was hard enough on the Camino to find the odd bush and a bit of privacy for a quick pee. The idea of managing diarrhoea was too awful to contemplate, so I dosed myself solidly with tablets and kept going.

Next morning I woke feeling worse. I'll just walk slowly. I did that for the eight kilometres through the green rolling hills into Villafranca. By then I felt awful. It was only ten in the morning, but perhaps I should find an albergue and see if I could stay. Or maybe I could bus the next bit. Villafranca was quite a large town and looked touristy. It was probably served by buses.

If I could just rest for a while. There was a park in the middle of town, so I found a bench and stretched out on it. There were plenty of people around who no doubt eyed me curiously. I didn't care. I probably looked like the town tramp. I felt rather like the town tramp. I sure didn't feel like going anywhere in a hurry. I'd just lie there for a bit and then see how the world looked. And if people stared and wondered, too bad.

After a while, an hour maybe, I decided yes, I could go on. My guidebook said that the next bit was the most spectacular of the whole Camino, so it seemed a shame to drive past it. But going on meant committing to twelve kilometres of the steepest, if most beautiful, path of the whole journey. No villages, no shops, no nothing on the way. Just a tough slog up and over a mountain. I thought if I reach a point where I can't go on, I'll just lay my sleeping bag down on the ground and stay there the night.

There was an alternative path along the road, not steep and considerably shorter. Why didn't I compromise with that? No, Wonder Woman can stride tall mountains no problem, even when her gut is in turmoil and her legs feel like jelly.

So I set off, slowly. A German pilgrim passed me almost immediately, then Liam, a young Irish man, caught up and started to walk with me. I suggested he go on, but he was happy to walk at my pace and welcomed the company over the mountain. Not that I was much company. I'd think funny clever things in my head, but didn't have the energy to make them come out my mouth. Liam chatted on regardless. And I made those mechanical kinds of responses my kids used to call 'mummy talk'.

Each step took total concentration and a huge effort of will. We climbed steeply, each turn bringing new vistas of the mountains all around. We decided to have a break when we got to the highest point and getting there took forever. No doubt the views were spectacular but I was in no state to enjoy them. I willed my jelly legs to keep going and the contents of my gut to stay inside my body. And they did. Just.

And then we went down. That was steep too and we thought we'd lost the path at one point. Finally, finally, we arrived at Tradobelo. I collapsed into a bed and awoke a couple of hours later thinking that I would probably never move again. My head was aching and my body shivering and I thought there was a good chance I'd contribute one more memorial cross to the Camino. So much for Wonder Woman.

'Have a wonderful time'

I did have a wonderful time in all sorts of ways. One of the best was meeting so many people from so many backgrounds. And telling our stories to each other. My first little fear, that I would find no one to speak to, proved groundless. Most afternoons, most nights, there were conversations. Surprising conversations. Like on the second night. There was a restaurant offering a special menu peregrino and I went with Sinh, the Korean student I'd walked with that day. She spoke little English and I spoke no Korean but we got on well enough. We were joined by a German language teacher, and an Iranian paediatrician who spoke several languages. He said that after the first few, learning another one is easy.

We got talking about language and culture and thinking and how they are connected. And the theories. Does language shape our ideas or do our experiences determine language? Is there any significance in the fact that in English we use the one word to express our 'love' – of football, of ice cream, or of our newborn child? Or that in Spanish the same word is used to address God and any man?

***

Not only the people. There were wonderful things to be seen, experiences to be had. Spanish churches are strong, solid things which dominate the towns and villages. With often a square steeple, not tapering, but rising solidly into the sky. Next to the albergue in Logrono was a massive church with an equally massive bell tower, except it had no bell. In that space where a bell should be, a pair of storks had built a nest; a penthouse apartment towering above the city.

Not to be outdone, another pair had built their huge, twiggy nest on the roof of the others'. The stork in the top nest was just mooching about, but the lower nest had two chicks peeping out from time to time. Which led me to wonder, who brings stork babies?

***

There's supposed to be something special about hearing the first cuckoo of spring. There was certainly something special about hearing the first cuckoo of my life. Outside of a cuckoo clock that is. On and on it went, chiming more hours than I cared to count. And no mechanical whirr to set it going.

***

It was a long walk into Portomarin with one final challenge at the end. Like something Bunyan's Pilgrim might have encountered. The only way into the town was up a huge flight of concrete stairs. They probably led to the Celestial City, but you couldn't be sure from below. So up I plodded. It was best not to look up, but just take one step, then the next.

At the top were four young men accosting pilgrims. Selling something probably. Maybe handing out leaflets for a new albergue, though four seemed unnecessary for that. Peddling religion, perhaps, or mobile phones. I was a little wary. The stairs had been enough. I didn't need the challenge of fending off persistent hawkers.

Turns out they were a film crew from National Geographic, making a documentary on the Camino. Was I willing to be interviewed? Sure, why not. Portomarin was where I was headed that day and now I had nothing better to do. Besides, it was a good excuse to just sit for a while. Which I did at the top of those stairs. The sound man held his big fluffy microphone, the camera man pointed his camera, the interviewer asked his questions and the interpreter occasionally helped with a question or answer.

The interviewer said at the end that he had met a New Zealander who had the same sort of... He paused to find the word, which I thought would be 'accent'. But no, the same sort of energy. How curious. I wonder what he meant.

Another episode in my Big Adventure and such fun.

'Be or not be, there is no try'

Some days were just mud days. One involved a huge uphill trek through thick, sticky mud. The mud first, then a loose layer of small sharp pebbles. That was thick too. And slippery. Better, though, I thought. Until I came to a cyclist whose tyres, like my shoes, were coated with mud, his even thicker. And his mud was now studded with pebbles, his wheels like two circles of rich plum pudding, so thick they couldn't turn, so he was doing his best to scrape it off. I made sympathetic noises, but he consoled himself with the thought 'more merit for me'.

Is that what it's all about? No pain no gain? You could buy T-shirts that said that. I didn't want one. I didn't like that idea.

***

If I was going to be grumpy anywhere it would have been at Burgos. It had been a hot, miserable walk into the city and the small albergue in the middle of town was full by the time I arrived. So I walked another two kilometres to the big one on the outskirts of town. No kitchen, no sitting room, no shop, cold showers and about a hundred pilgrims crammed into a little wooden hotbox of a building. I sat outside under the trees. There was nowhere else to sit. I could see the late afternoon sun beaming on to the wall. The wall which had my bunk on the other side of it.

I wasn't about to be Pollyanna-ish and find things to be glad about. But neither did I want to mope and grump. I decided to just be in the situation and that would be enough. And it was.

***

I arrived at Trabadelo sick with a gastric bug. Despite my Wonder

Woman aspirations, I rested there an extra day, willing my gut to return to normal. And my energy level. And that's about all I did.

I let go of striving, and just allowed myself to be, something I don't find easy. The albergue was clean and comfortable and for most of the day I had it all to myself. A gentle setting for the lesson of non-trying. Of just being.

'vaya con dios'

My guidebook said it was worth taking the detour, so I did. It meant an extra two kilometres, but that wasn't too bad. The little church at Eunate was all by itself in the middle of nowhere. It was roughly round in shape, less massive than most Spanish churches, and surrounded by a colonnade. I was there too early so didn't get to see inside, which was a shame. The story is that there was once a burial ground alongside, for pilgrims whose journey ended rather more suddenly and permanently than they had expected.

They don't have special burial grounds now, but pilgrims still die en route. In the first four days, I passed four memorials. It's something I'd thought about. Somehow the Camino reminds us of our life pilgrimage and its ultimate destination. Those symbols of death brought me no sense of a life beyond. I can't know and it doesn't matter. All I can do is live the best life I can. And that may well be all there is.

***

Cemeteries in Spain are discreetly tucked away behind high walls, well out of the villages. But I passed one whose message was anything but subtle. Carved into the wall above the entry was as sign that translated something like 'I was once what you are, you will one day be what I am'. Indeed.

***

God plays a greater or lesser part in each person's Camino. As she walked, Julie, the wholesome schoolteacher from California, had earphones and an iPod and listened to sermons about the Bible. Having God along, downloaded from the internet, was an important part of her Camino.

***

And the God stories along the way. The Spanish like their miracles. In the church at O'Cebeiro there's a chalice and paten on display in a glass cabinet. The story goes that an arrogant, but world-weary, priest was reluctant to give communion to a man he considered ignorant and unworthy, but who was, in fact, devout and holy in the extreme.

This worthiness was acted out one communion time when the bread and wine did rather more than the usual transubstantiation. In front of the holy man it was transformed into the real body and blood of Jesus Christ. And the vessels in which this miracle occurred, the chalice and the paten, are preserved in the church till this day, physical evidence of the miracle. There for the edification of the faithful and the curiosity of the tourists

Good story but my guidebook gave only a few tantalising details. Was it a re-constituted mini Jesus (or indeed a full-size Jesus) that appeared or was it just bits of flesh and blood in the separate vessels? And what happened next? Sadly, those questions remain for me unanswered.

'Feliz viajes'

Some things were distinctly Spanish. The countryside for a start. The path was sometimes overlaid by roads and highways, and sometimes it was a thin little track. Passing through mountains and clear rivers, vineyards and farmland in neat textured patchworks of greens and golds, and thick, dark forests right out of my childhood fantasies. Forests where you might meet Goldilocks and Red Riding Hood and any number of fairy tale characters. And, every few kilometres, the villages, unchanged for centuries, with their old, old buildings and their narrow angled streets.

***

So many windmills. They fringed most skylines. The high ones anyway, and there were plenty of those. A latter-day Don Quixote would find much to tilt at. I wonder if we need one?

***

The walk to El Burgo Ranero was mercifully short. I could have gone another thirteen kilometres to the next village but I chose not to do that.

When I arrived at the albergue, the hospitalero warned me that there was a fiesta in town that night. And that meant loud music and revelry till goodness knows when. At least, I think that's what he said. He deterred some others who shook their heads gravely and decided that an extra thirteen kilometres was a better option.

Can a fiesta be any worse than a room full of snoring pilgrims? Except for the fireworks at some early hour, it wasn't. I inserted my trusty earplugs and slept through the lot.

I'm not sure what the fiestas are celebrating other than providing a good excuse for a wild old party. I was in a restaurant one night with the television on and they gave a fiesta forecast along with the weather. Tomorrow you can expect fiestas in…

***

Given Spaniards' laid-back approach to many things, they're surprisingly rigid about time. The locals eat at around ten but many restaurants provided a special 'menu peregrino' at an earlier time. A specified time. Seven means seven, if that's when it was. If you arrived two minutes earlier, they would say 'Siente!' in a highly affronted tone and leave you standing outside the empty dining room until the clock said precisely that. Then and only then were you allowed in to sit and be served.

'Climb every mountain'

Plenty of mountains right from day one with steep, rocky, muddy tracks. The view from the top was worth it. And the sense of achievement. Trouble is, once you go up you have to come down again.

***

Lots of the up and down kind, but some mountains were horizontal. The walk across the meseta into Calzadilla de la Cueza was flat and hot. Seventeen kilometres without a village when, until then, there was one every few kilometres.

The route was an old Roman road, straight and flat, the landscape relatively featureless. Not featureless by Nullarbor Plain standards, but certainly by the Camino's. It felt like a mountain laid out flat on the ground that just had to be got over. And get over it I did.

I was starting to flag and had begun to sing a little walking song to keep myself going when suddenly there it was. Mostly the villages were clearly visible in the distance, like Dorothy's Oz, their presence providing its own encouragement. But this one just popped up out of nowhere – right at the foot of that horizontal mountain. And very welcome it was too.

***

The highest point on the Camino, fifteen hundred metres, has an iron cross atop a tall wooden pole. And around the base, a hill of rocks and stones and other objects left by pilgrims.

I don't know what impulse leads us to build mounds of stones, but it's something pilgrims do all along the Camino. And there, at the highest point, the biggest mound of all.

I had visited central Australia a few years before, and picked up a red desert stone. I tucked it into my bag when I'd left home thinking to add it to the Camino mound. My little red stone from the heart of Australia. It was to be a sacred moment.

I stood, holding the stone in my hand, reflecting on the meaning of it all, when along came Leo. He was a jolly, chatty Dutch man and I'd told him about my stone. He offered to take a photo of me adding it to the pile.

It wasn't what I had in mind, but it seemed ungracious to refuse. So I said, Fine, but just give me a moment. I cradled it a few seconds more then walked up the mound and placed it right at the base of the pole, conscious of the camera all the while.

When it was done I was able to sit and know the moment. I cried some, I'm not sure why. It may be that I saw all life's connections and separations – people, places, things, dreams, aspirations – there in those stones. Stones and other objects, strange things, broken glasses, a loaf of bread. All brought from somewhere and placed in that great mound. Then those who leave them move on.

***

Having reached the highest point, I had to come down again. Mountains are like that. I left Manjarin in thick mist. The surrounding mountains may as well not have been. And maybe they weren't. Does a mountain exist if you can't see it? My world that morning was a clear little circle that moved along with me. Beyond that the mist. Nothing more. Except the steep, rocky path. Or at least the bits of path trapped within my moving circle. Then the mist cleared and the mountains returned.

'Walk cheerfully all the way'

George Fox said that. Not that exactly. What he said was, Walk cheerfully over the world answering that of God in every person. Every Quaker can tell you that. It's not easy, though. With some people, even with some pilgrims, answering their that-of-God can be quite a challenge.

Take Big Red Rita. She was tall, very tall, with wild blonde hair and sharp sunburnt features. A fresh red scab on her nose where she'd fallen or walked into something. She wore a red Basque beret and red leg-warmers. And she was loud and dominated every conversation in German, French and English.

And Marie Frances, the Canadian woman who complained about everything. Her pack was too heavy, the slopes were too steep, her companions too slow, twenty kilometres was too far for one day but, no, she didn't want to catch a bus for any of it.

At Torres del Rio it was a tall German man who strode into the albergue, plonked two bottles of red wine down on the table, and announced, 'This is dinner.' He confessed that he'd only walked forty kilometres that day instead of his usual fifty to sixty. Someone had stolen his boots and he had to break in a new pair. There was something about him I found disturbing. A driven, haunted look, like an addicted gambler.

And the sixty-something Italian man who stripped down to his jocks when he arrived at an albergue, and strutted around so clad (or so unclad) until dinner. He seemed not the least embarrassed. I was embarrassed enough for both of us.

Perhaps he had only one set of clothes and needed to wash them every day. Or his wife did, more likely. One night I saw him bathing and massaging her feet ever so tenderly. I forgave him a lot for that.

At Sahadun it was a succession of male cyclists striding into the albergue late afternoon in their loud, confident way, dripping sweat and testosterone. I know that peregrinos come in all shapes and sizes, but I found that lot a bit overwhelming.

***

At Granon and the next night at Tosantos I stayed at parish albergues. These are supported by the local church and run by volunteers, the pilgrims being charged 'a donation'. Dinner and breakfast were provided, although the pilgrims helped with the labour.

On both these nights the Italians took over. They were loud. They made up only a quarter of the numbers, but they took up ninety per cent of the airspace. At dinner they sat at one end of the table, laughing and talking all at once in that Italian way. Down the other end, we buttoned-up Anglos and Teutonics sat sedately, raising our eyebrows and discreetly rolling our eyes at the jollity going on down the Italian end. Not that they would have noticed, or cared. In fact, eventually one of them brought some of their wine down to us. Probably hoping to liven up the bunch of miserable old gits down the other end.

***

The albergue at Molinaseca opened into a square kitchen space with steps (or long seats) leading down to the central work area from all four sides. The décor was all black. Very Japanese.

I was preparing my dinner of stir-fried vegetables. A young woman was there preparing food also. Unlike me, she was taking a great deal of trouble. She pierced the bases of two containers of yogurt, partially peeled back the lids, then inverted the tubs, balancing them carefully over some glasses. Presumably to let the whey drain off. It was that important.

She spent ages beating and beating a mixture of I don't know what. She eventually added the yogurt and beat some more. There weren't many dishes in the cupboard, but she found one that would do, carefully arranged a layer of cake fingers over the base then spread the beaten mixture on top. Quite a procedure. Then she went off with this splendid dish. To the other albergue up the road a bit. How odd. Maybe she had friends staying there and was joining them for a shared meal, taking her contribution with her.

I returned to the kitchen after my meal, in time to see her putting the lid on the dirty pot before shoving it, unwashed, under the cupboard. Then she picked up her bag and headed back towards the other albergue. I didn't see her again.

I was angry all the next day. Why? It didn't inconvenience me in any way. I didn't need the pot or the space she was taking up in the kitchen. With every other pilgrim I'd met, even those with odd quirks and funny ways, there was a sense of us supporting each other. We looked to see what the other might need, be it company, silence, wine, food, or first aid. Her action seemed such a desecration of that. I wanted to say to her, you're not a real pilgrim. Go home and grow up and come back when you're ready to do it right.

But perhaps that's the point. Who knows what she was to learn from her Camino? Or, indeed, what I was to learn from mine.

I heard later that the hospitalero there had been rude to some pilgrims, so maybe there was a private little agenda being played out that I knew nothing about.

***

It wasn't difficult to see that of God in Andy. But he denied the goodness in himself. He didn't fit any of my pilgrim categories. Self-confessed crook, he'd spent much of his formative years in Borstal and lived for years in the United States avoiding arrest by the British police. Or so he said. Self-confessed alcoholic, and he certainly demolished several bottles of wine in the short time I spoke with him. Despite all that, there was a goodness to him which he resisted any suggestion of.

***

I thought of them all, all those difficult ones, from time to time as I walked and held them in the Light. A Quaker thing to do. If we know of someone who is in trouble (or perhaps who is trouble, though we're too nice to say that out loud) we ask each other to 'hold them in the Light'. Though, in my twenty-plus years with Quakers, I've never thought to ask another Friend how they do that. Nor has anyone asked me. It wasn't until last year when I read a novel by the English writer, Patrick Gale, that I even thought to wonder. He describes how his various Quaker characters do that holding. And then I wondered.

For me it's not really visual. It's something like the Buddhist Loving Kindness meditation, only without the words and the structure. But it's not quite that either. It's more than an attitude of loving kindness. It's also, for me, imagining the person being suffused with some kind of mystical light. Divine, if you like. I don't know that it changes anything for those held, but it certainly changes me the holder. And that's not such a bad thing.

'Shalom, dear friend'

I felt something of an alien arriving all alone in Madrid, my pilgrim persona at odds with the urban activities around me. My stick helped. People looked at it and wondered. And sometimes couldn't help asking. Or commenting. I felt welcomed.

***

The pilgrims greeted each other along the way – Hola! Which is pretty much Shalom. And sometimes that was all. Or we might walk together for an hour or a day, or share a meal, or a night crammed together in our bunks. We were a mixed lot – age, nationality, motivation – but we all had the Camino look: walking clothes, backpack, cockle shell and a stick or even two. But it was more than the 'look' that bound us together. We had all chosen to be pilgrims, walking out our own personal search. For something. Shalom to us all.

***

The albergue at Granon was part of the church building. And the church business. I'd heard of it. One of the places you must stay. The staircase angled its way up through the old building. Quite a long way. Two women, volunteers, greeted me with a big soft chair and a glass of water before getting on with the business. That was nice, not to be rushed.

That first level was the living space. A tiny kitchen and a large open area with lounge chairs and pictures and shelves of books. An open fire place. Not that we needed it that night. And then, upstairs in the loft, the sleeping space. It was like a large attic, the roof sloping down to the floor on two sides. No beds as such. Just thin mats jammed edge to edge along the floor. Brown vinyl. No pillows and no blankets that I could see.

There were forty-one of us there that night. We helped set up trestle tables, but there was no room in the kitchen. The two workers could barely fit in, so the food preparation was all done by them. For the forty-one of us. We ate at two long tables, with conversations going on in half a dozen languages and a sense of being pilgrims together.

There was a film crew there as well, just passing through, though I only got to see them from a distance. Making a documentary on the Camino, someone said. I caught up with them some weeks later and found out more.

Sleeping a metre away from total strangers had been something of a challenge. Here it was more like a millimetre away. I filled my ears with earplugs and slept oblivious to the chorus of snores. Which I may well have contributed to.

They still call it a hospital and it is a place of hospitality. We'd walked through the day, singly or in groups, at different speeds and from different places, and come together here, to eat, drink and be jolly. Then to rest the night and start off again in the morning to whatever destinations the new day would bring. That's what pilgrims do.

Payment was by donation. Most such places had a box with a slot for the contributions, but this box was open. With a sign in several languages: leave what you can, take what you need. That's hospitality.

***

The village of Santibanez was too small to have a shop of its own. Or a restaurant. The albergue was tiny too, but it did provide an evening meal. Fortunately.

It was a little old house with three small bedrooms downstairs and more upstairs. I didn't go up to see. The shower and toilet were outside and there was an overgrown orchard out the back. And we were a quiet lot there that night.

In the afternoon, some of us gathered under the trees, reading, sewing or just sitting, mostly in silence. Then, after the meal, someone played a guitar and someone else a flute. Someone sang a bit. The rest of us sat around and drank red wine and listened.

***

The albergue at Manjarin is perched all by itself high in the mountains. There may once have been a village, but now there's nothing. Except the mountains and the albergue. It's not a place for the faint hearted. There's no electricity. No showers at all, not even cold ones. No water, in fact. Well, there was a fuente (fountain) a hundred metres or so down the hill. Freezing cold, the pool full of green slime with a warning 'no potable' sign beside it. I decided to give my daily cleaning ritual a miss.

The toilet was a rickety little construction up the hill in the other direction. A raised wooden platform with a flimsy fence around and a few boards removed. You squatted over the hole and there was a container of lime to sprinkle in. Another bucket to deposit your used toilet paper. The whole system guaranteed to induce constipation in all but the most adventurous.

The place was run by some modern-day Knights Templar. Whether authorised or self-appointed, I don't know. Their manner was serious and they wore bandanas with a distinctive red cross, the Templars' insignia.

Dinner was provided. No shops or bars here or anywhere handy. About twelve pilgrims, most of them male.

Monica, from the US, had just begun her pilgrimage, with that vitality and directness some Americans have. She was studying Spanish and the Camino was an assignment. She was to keep a journal, in Spanish, so had a strong sense of purpose.

Kat was there to have fun. Kat was Danish and was walking with Monica. She'd come on impulse and the two of them were struggling a bit.

They'd met on a holiday last year and had got on well. But walking the Camino with someone is a different thing. Your rhythms matter. And your choices. Whether you get going early or late, the pace you walk at, where you stop and for how long, what you stop for, whether you chat or walk in silence. They all matter. They matter a lot. And little things can chafe. After just a couple of days, the chafing was obvious between Monica and Kat. Like blisters that you know are only going to get worse. Little niggly comments. Only joking. But not really.

I heard later they'd gone their separate ways. You can't do much on the Camino without it getting around. We were each other's news.

There were four teenage boys that night at Manjarin, apparently there for their own good, under the care of a couple of guardians. The good hadn't yet become obvious, at least not to them. We couldn't talk, but one of them especially looked determinedly glum. I was glad they weren't my travelling companions. They would have been hard work. Prisoners used to be able to walk the Camino instead of serving their sentence in jail and it felt rather like that.

And a few miscellaneous others. All male.

We crowded around the table in the little kitchen. Dinner by candlelight; there was no other choice. In unavoidable intimacy, with our various tensions and no common language.

It turned out to be a most companionable evening. One of those times when I felt like a real pilgrim. There was a young Ecuadorean man with flashing good looks and a warmth of manner. He had us go around the table and tell our names and where we were from. More than that we were unable to share, at least not with language. But we laughed a lot at our various attempts. It was a good thing to do.

During the meal, Monica sat beside me working up indignation about who was likely to be left with the cleaning up. So, after we'd eaten, she took the matter in hand and organised us all. Especially the men. This turned out to be heaps of fun as shifts were timed and we jostled each other for our turn with wash brushes and tea towels. All done in no time.

We slept in an old stone building. Thin mattresses side by side on a raised platform and more up the ladder in a loft. The night was cold up there in the mountains, so being packed in together wasn't such a bad thing. I was glad the albergues weren't all like that. Some took one look and passed it by. But I was glad I stayed.

I was resting under a tree the next day when the handsome Ecuadorean came jogging by. Obviously in a hurry to be somewhere. He realised who I was and jogged back to greet me, kissing me warmly on the hand. He too must have felt the bond that formed between the motley little group that we were. It was a special night.

'Feliz viaje, disfrutade la exexperiencia y q'ue tus stenes se hogan realisted'

I left home not knowing quite what this message said, so it was the one to go to when reflecting on times of doubt or confusion.

There were many times when I didn't understand the words that were spoken, but could pick up the gist of what was said. A bit like the Swedish chef on *The Muppets*. He didn't say real words, but his intonation, inflection, body movement and facial expression (even though the eyebrows were the only moveable part) conveyed so much. And so it was at times on the Camino. But not always. Sometimes it was just a torrent of words that told me nothing.

***

One night there were four of us around a dinner table. It was like one of those logic puzzles. A is from Slovenia and B is from Poland, but they can understand each other. B also speaks Italian, as does C, who speaks English as well. A also speaks English and D speaks only English (guess who D was). How can A, B, C and D hold a conversation? Well, they did, and a mighty fine one at that.

***

I felt embarrassed on behalf of my fellow Australians. Almost everyone I met from elsewhere spoke two or more languages at least passably well. And here we are stuck in our complacent little monolingual world. It's so parochial of us and a bit smug too.

'Courage, pilgrim'

Even the plane trip from Australia asked for courage. The sheer endurance factor for a start, through a long, long night as we travelled west, doing our best to outrun the sun and stretch the night as far as we could. I can be an anxious flyer and I didn't like it when the pilot warned of coming turbulence. Apparently there was 'weather'. It lasted quite a while and was scary enough, though the pilot's grave warning had me expecting worse.

***

There were days when I questioned the whole thing. What was I doing here?

My sister, Pat, had rung before I left Australia, asking why I was going. I didn't really know. On the Camino, just out from Logrono, I was asking myself the same question. I had met so many people who seemed driven. To go as hard and as fast as was humanly possible, to meet some sort of macho challenge or to earn most spiritual merit. Did I really want to spend five more weeks doing that?

But then, walking, I came to know that other purposes were other people's. This was my Camino. I mightn't know why I was doing it, but I was doing it. Why didn't matter. I would just walk through the Spanish countryside and feel the serenity of that. Feel it seep into me. That was enough.

Sometimes I thought of John Bunyan's Pilgrim and wondered what life allegories I was walking out as I went.

***

The walk into Leon was scary. Along the edge of a main road with a steady stream of cars and trucks hurtling towards you at high speed. A momentary lapse of concentration on someone's part and there'd be one fewer pilgrim on the Camino.

***

By the time I got to Portomarin I'd had enough of albergues. At least the big, crowded municipal ones. The dormitory was more crowded than any I'd been in. The big, modern kitchen had two small frying pans, a dozen plates, and a lot of empty cupboards. No saucepans, no cutlery, no cooking utensils, nothing to drink from. Courage, Kez! It did only cost three euros.

'Where's your strength?'

Our feet and legs preoccupied us. So many pilgrims pushed themselves too far too fast and suffered blisters or inflamed tendons or joints. I'd see them hobbling along the path or around the albergues at night and be grateful. Grateful for my own healthy body. I travelled not too far or too fast, but through to the end, with few complaints.

Some pilgrims would say things like 'I've worn these boots for six years without problems, but now I have the most terrible blisters'. My shoes were light, flexible and water-repellent; I wore two pairs of socks, one thick and one wicking; I stretched and exercised my feet; I walked a moderate distance each day; I carried a light pack. Is that what it takes or did I just have the good fortune to be born with robust foot genes? Nature or nurture, I don't know.

***

Was I too cautious, walking only twenty kilometres a day? When I did just a little more, I felt the extra distance. One such day was from Cadzadilla de la Cueza to Sahagun. Not particularly hard. But for the last few kilometres I needed to sing myself a rousing walking song to pick up my pace and keep going. When I did make it to the albergue, I slept for the afternoon. It was no small thing to ask of my ageing body, to walk even that far every day for thirty-seven days. But I did it.

***

It's hard sometimes to know if something is a strength or a weakness. I've been a vegetarian a long time now. Partly because I'm squeamish about blood. I look the other way when I pass a butcher shop. But also, it just feels a gentler way of being.

I knew this would be a challenge on the Camino. Vegetarianism is almost unknown in the villages of northern Spain. Many restaurants had a special 'menu peregrino', three courses, a limited choice, plus wine, all for around eight to ten euros. If you made a fuss (and if you could make your dilemma understood) you would probably get fried eggs and chips as a second course. But it was usually done reluctantly and with bad grace. What was I to do?

I decided to go for the coward's way and just choose the least meaty options. I tried not to think about what I was eating. Like a child might with Brussels sprouts. Chew it, swallow it. That's it.

Not Bron. She was a real vegetarian. She stuck to her principles and insisted every time. Or cooked for herself. She said I wasn't a real vegetarian if I was prepared to eat meat. I guess she was right.

In Spanish there are two forms of the verb to be, which is confusing but probably useful. You can use the two verbs, soy or estoy, to say 'I am'. I haven't got it totally sorted. It's something to do with the quality in question. Is it of your essence or is it something more ephemeral? I think, when we said I am vegetarian, Bron was the one and I the other.

I liked Bron. She was my most constant walking companion. She was slight, darkly tanned, wore skimpy clothes, and piled her hair in astonishing knots on top of her head. Sometimes one tall one, sometimes a cluster of them. She'd sung in an anarchist punk band in the seventies, slept on friends' couches when she was young and pregnant, and sent her son to Summerhill. She smoked lots but was giving it up. Soon. Pushing sixty, she was now more or less respectable. Now an artist. Still very pure. She grows her food in a community plot in London and is unswervingly vegetarian.

I wasn't. One night I ordered fried calamari, thinking of those innocuous crumbed rings you get in Australia. What came on my plate was a whole squid, accusing in its white nakedness. I squirm as I think of it. Is that a strength or a weakness?

***

I'd often start off walking in the cool of the morning and had a thin little cardigan that was just perfect for then. I only needed to wear it until the day warmed up. Or I warmed up. But, it was such a bother taking my pack off, I found a way of wriggling out of my cardigan with the pack in place. A minor Houdini act I practised each day. Not without cost, though. My efforts progressively tore the stitching under the arms. So I bought a needle and thread and sat quietly one afternoon repairing the damage. What a delight that was, just sitting and stitching, slowly and carefully. Totally focused.

It was such a pleasure that I went searching for a needlework shop in Leon. Found one and bought myself a little cross-stitch kit. I could then sit and sew of an afternoon when, otherwise, I might just sit. I'm not much good at just sitting. I don't know if that's a strength or a weakness.

By the end I was doing that more. Just sitting. I don't know whether I learned a Camino lesson or whether I'd just got tired and even sewing was an unnecessary effort.

***

I became obsessive about being clean. One night, in an albergue high in the mountains, there was no shower; no washing facilities at all. I couldn't wait to wash off my travel grime at Molinaseca the next day. It was more than cleaning off the grime that had gathered on my body from outside. I felt there were bad humours oozing out of me like body toxins in a sauna. Though these were more of a spiritual nature. Camino as sauna for the soul.

In my Catholic childhood we were told that our sins caused ugly stains and spots to appear on our souls, but that the grace of Confession would make them bright and shiny again. Like a sacramental laundry detergent.

It felt like those spots and stains on my soul were working their way out as I walked. If I didn't wash them off, they'd accumulate there on my skin, or maybe soak back in again. So I really needed that ritual cleansing every day. I could see the satisfaction in baptism by immersion. I did it for myself each day on the Camino. Would anyone notice on my return, that I'd rid myself of some of my nastier bits? Though perhaps it was those deep, secret nasties that sloughed off.

Those mean little bits that can lurk behind a kind and positive surface. Have they gone? How will I know? Maybe they'd just come to the surface.

Or perhaps my washing had more to do with comfort. Not just the comfort of a clean body. The comfort of something constant when so much was changing. The rhythm of washing myself and washing my clothes each day. No matter what else changed, that was there, every day.

'To travel hopefully is a better thing than to arrive'

We all went at our own pace, choosing how far and how quickly we would walk each day. For some, the arriving was the important thing – the quicker the better. The first day I went as fast as could, anxious that I might not get there in time. I arrived at Zubiri by midday long before the cheap albergue opened. Exhausted and wanting only to shower and sleep.

After that I relaxed a little and went more slowly. Walked more slowly and stopped at places along the way. Took time to just be. The going, not just the arriving, was of value. I might never arrive, or the arriving might not bring what I'd hoped. I might as well relish the journey.

After a long and muddy climb, I paused before entering the village of Maneru to scrape at least some of the mud from my shoes. A local couple approached much agitated, insisting I follow another route, not the marked one, through the town. There was no arguing, so I set off their way. But with no Camino markings it was all wrong. I felt lost. When they had safely gone, I snuck back into the village and followed the comforting arrows.

I think they were telling me to walk along the road. Quicker, cleaner, more direct. But walking along a main road is a very different experience to walking cross country, following an ancient path. Sometimes muddy, sometimes rocky, sometimes steep. My fellow travellers the pilgrims I could see before and behind me. And those I couldn't see. Those who had followed the trail for all those centuries before and those who will follow on for however long into the future. That was the line I was part of. That was the path I wanted to follow, however much mud. Besides, the Camino isn't about avoiding adversity. It's about facing it and dealing with it as best you can.

But I couldn't explain all that with my fifty words of Spanish.

***

While my guidebook gave the distance between villages, I had little sense of how I was going overall. Until the mileage posts appeared. One at three hundred and seventy-five kilometres, another at one hundred and ninety-five. Yes, I was making it. The hope of arriving seemed more realistic, less flimsy. I might actually get there.

Sarria was a special milepost. It's one hundred and eleven kilometres from Santiago. Pilgrims can start there and still get a certificate, a compostela. So arriving there meant this was really the last bit. My hope had wavered at times, but there was always enough to keep me going.

***

I expected to get more excited as I neared Santiago, but each day was just another day to be walked. Until the last day. That felt different. My mother had a wise saying for every occasion. One was Anticipation is better than realisation. We lose that as we get older: the anticipation of Christmas or birthdays. Perhaps we protect ourselves from disappointment. Better not to expect too much. We miss out on something, becoming so jaded.

The good thing is that some realisations can take you by surprise, with their unexpected delights. I wondered what Santiago would bring.

***

Thirty-nine days after I set off from Roncesvalles, I arrived in Santiago. That morning, my last walking day, I did wake up with a growing bubble of excitement and anticipation.

After wandering through Santiago I finally found the cathedral. Inside, it felt like just another cathedral. No bells, no whistles, no great surge of emotion. There were people all around and a sign requesting silence. There was no great rush of devotion for Saint James – or for anyone else for that matter.

So I went outside and sat in one of the adjoining squares. That was better. Other pilgrims arriving or sitting or wandering about, some looking dazed. One standing against the cathedral wall, singing aloud his own personal alleluia, unaware of and uncaring about any human audience. We pilgrims were an odd assorted lot, but we accepted each others' oddness. No one minded him in the least.

I sat for some time just knowing that I was there and savouring that. I had achieved my goal, completed my pilgrimage. Done what I had set out to do. But there was no trumpet fanfare. Just a quiet sense of achievement. Job done, on time and under budget.

I found somewhere to stay and washed off the last bit of Camino grime. Then back for another go at the cathedral. But I just didn't want to do the traditional pilgrim things. I might have put my hands into the worn-down hand marks in the Tree of Jesse, but I couldn't find it. The place where I expected it to be was cordoned off for repairs. There was a long queue waiting to climb the stairs and hug the statue of St James and I didn't want to do that. I don't think I'd have done it anyway, queue or no queue. Nor did I want to go down into the crypt to venerate, or even pass by, whose ever bones are lying there. It's unlikely they are the apostle's and, even if they were, so what. I saw the giant swinging incense burner, but they now only get that going on special occasions. Modern-day pilgrims are a cleaner, less smelly lot than they used to be. Not so much need to mask their smell with incense.

No, one thing's for sure. For me the Camino had little to do with St James. He's sometimes shown as Moor-slayer. Hardly something to celebrate. Sometimes as pilgrim, which I find mysterious. If the Camino is pilgrimage to St James, how does he as pilgrim fit into that? His is a good story but not one that, in the end, I wanted to buy into.

Perhaps the travelling was more important than the arriving. Though it was good to arrive.

'Have fun!'

One day I stopped for lunch at a little park on the edge of a village. Grass, a few trees, tables and benches. I'd just settled in and was starting to eat when two busloads of children arrived. A group of them clustered around my table. We had a great time, exchanging names and greetings in Spanish and English. Eating our lunch together. They seemed to enjoy that: sharing a picnic table with a foreign peregrina. I enjoyed it too.

***

Coming into Belorado I was ready for a break. Just there, at the entrance to the village, was a little park with tables and benches. Looked a bit dilapidated, but should do the trick. Or so I thought. I took off my pack and sat down on one of the benches. It was attached to a table, but neither the bench nor the table stayed attached to the ground.

The whole thing tipped over, landing me flat on my back in the gravel. I lay there laughing at the indignity of it all. I told myself it was just a matter of rolling over and I could get to my feet again. Which wouldn't have been so easy with a backpack on. I would have been as helpless as an upturned beetle. But, as it was, no harm was done and a good deal of fun was had. A shame there was no one there to share the joke.

***

There was time and freedom to enjoy childish things for the sheer fun of it. I sat in the churchyard at Ages, still and alone, then on the way back to the albergue, passed a children's playground. There was no one around and the urge was too great. The swing was irresistible and I swung and swung in simple delight.

***

I don't know what people did with their sex lives on the Camino. Those who have sex lives. There were just open fields, bars, churches, and the albergues with their communal sleeping arrangements. No obvious place for liaisons. They probably existed, but, like public toilets and post offices, remained a mystery to me.

There was a young Italian couple on their honeymoon. They slept very chastely in separate bunks in a room full of strangers. And a French couple, status unknown, who slept very unchastely in the same bunk in a room full of strangers. There were other couples too, some long term and some from the Camino. I guess they worked something out.

I had dinner one night with a young Korean student and a business man, strangers all. We said goodnight and went our separate ways, the student and I to our shared albergue, the man to his hotel. I met the two of them again two days later. Now they were a 'we' and were travelling together. But then, in another few days, I met him, all alone once more. I was too discreet to ask, 'Where is your little Korean friend?' but I was curious. It was like missing an episode of *Days of Our Lives* or *Big Brother*. We were living our own mobile soap opera, providing interest and entertainment for each other.

We had none of the usual entertainment. No television, radio, newspapers, magazines. Just the occasional book. So, like Chaucer's pilgrims on their way to Canterbury, we had to live out and tell our little life dramas – or comedies or farces – to entertain each other along the way.

'Think red cordial!'

This message jumped out at me when reflecting on my more bizarre experiences. At one stop I was chatted up by a German guy with an American accent, the result of twenty years in Honolulu. I felt an unlikely pick-up: sweaty, bedraggled, sunburnt. Not my most attractive. But he paid for my beer and invited me to sit at his table with his three German buddies. Turns out he was more interested in my soul than my body.

He was a ukulele-playing born-again Christian and the price of my beer was a little sermon or two. A reasonable transaction. The four of them had booked their Camino through a travel agent. They were waiting for the car to pick them up and take them to their hotel for the night. No crowded albergues for them.

Mr Born-Again was the first of many Germans to tell me of the popular comedian who had written a best-seller about his Camino experiences. Since then Germans have been coming in droves. Apparently more Germans than any other group now walk the Camino.

***

One day on the hot, flat meseta, someone passed me. Not an uncommon event, but this one made me smile. He had the usual backpack, but lacked the usual stick. Instead, he held a big, blue umbrella over his head. Quite sensible, really, for the meseta, if a little unusual.

Looking odd didn't bother pilgrims on the whole. Except for the beautiful people, and there weren't too many of them. Though I saw one carefully shaving her legs one night. More often they didn't bother much with appearance. They'd walk the day with various bits of washing pinned to the outside of their pack. Got the clothes dry.

***

El Ganso was an old old village with many of its buildings crumbling away. There in the middle was The Cowboy Bar. It could have strayed from the set of a quirky comedy western. It was unlike anything else on the Camino. I was there early morning before it opened, but those who did get to see it said it was as bizarre on the inside as the outside promised.

'Are we there yet?'

The walk from Lorca was my first are-we-there-yet day. The day before had been long and hard; my feet hurt, my knees hurt, my buttocks hurt, and every step was an effort I didn't want to make. But I soon got over that. A shower, a rest, a sit on a shady hill. It was good to be there.

***

Burgos was another are-we-there-yet experience; hot, crowded, industrial. But the next day brought Hornillos del Camino. A cool albergue with only twelve to a room, hot showers, friendly hospitaleros. How little it takes to feel like heaven.

***

I don't think I'd run out of tolerance for albergues generally. The albergue experience changed in that last province of Galicia. The albergues changed, for a start. The municipal ones. They were all essentially the same and they were all essentially awful. They were clean – clinically clean – and they were cheap. That wasn't the problem. Their design seemed based on the question: how can we fit the greatest number of human bodies into the smallest possible space? Perhaps no one asked the question What will that experience be like for those human bodies? The answer would have been: awful. In them I felt like a newly-assigned battery hen badly in need of adjustment therapy.

The beds were metal-framed double bunks jammed together in pairs and lined up in rows with barely enough space to stand beside the bunks or walk between the rows. And in the tiny space between the bunks we needed to fit four backpacks and four human bodies doing whatever they needed to do with their packs, their belongings, their bed or themselves.

The shower cubicles were tiny and had no door or curtain of any kind. So the common area in the bathroom was likely to be full of bodies. In various stages of wetness, cleanness and clothedness. Jostling to deal with those states in the space outside the cubicles and between the hand basins.

That last part of the Camino became more and more crowded. This made the problem even greater. You can earn the certificate of completion, the compostela, if you walk the last hundred kilometres, and many, especially Spaniards, opt to do that. Besides it was July and into holiday time, and that meant even more people.

For someone who values privacy and personal space it was challenging. They'd soon have to trim my beak or I'd start pecking myself or my fellows. The trouble was there was not much in the way of alternatives. At least, not alternative albergues.

After three nights of these places I headed for a fourth. I couldn't do it. I stopped outside. Through the windows I could see those crammed rows of metal bunks and my soul just refused. I'd come as far as I'd intended to that day but I thought, I'm going to walk on and find something else. I don't know what or where and I don't care. I'm going on.

Just down the road was a kind of holiday resort. Newish with sprawling wooden buildings. I could have a room for thirty-two euros. Ten times what I would have paid at the albergue, but I would have paid a hundred times that night. Oh, the sheer bliss of having a room to myself, a bed to myself, a shower and toilet all to myself. A shower where you didn't have to keep pressing the button every ten seconds to keep the water flowing. Toilet paper. A big, soft, fluffy towel and a bed with real sheets. This must be what heaven is like.

'Pause to reflect'

I did that every day as part of my walking meditation. Then each afternoon I'd sit and ponder and write. And others did too. A quietly companionable thing to do.

***

On the way into Navarette were the ruins of a mediaeval monastery. Originally it provided care for pilgrims on their journey. Now it was just a curiosity. A few crumbling walls. Something to look at. Somewhere to sit. Somewhere to graffiti if that's what you wanted. And some did. I sat for a while in the ruins and thought of all the pilgrims who had sought haven there. And all the pilgrims since who had passed by or rested there. So many. And I was one of them.

***

I'm not much of a beer drinker. Not usually. But I really enjoyed it on those hot days. Once I had settled into an albergue and showered and changed, to find a bar and sit, with a big glass of cold beer. Sometimes by myself, sometimes not. And reflected on the day. Life had become simple and the pleasures of small things very great. Even unaccustomed things like a glass of cold beer at the end of a hot day.

***

Of course there had to be ducks. Ducks mean something – I'm not sure what – in my spiritual journey. And I found some. My Camino ducks.

A few years ago I was on a Quaker retreat. Two nights and one day of it were totally silent. At least, they were supposed to be. On the silent afternoon I walked in bushland near the retreat centre and sat to rest beside a pond. A family of ducks appeared, mum, dad and a whole host of littlies. They came towards me, perhaps looking for food. I confess. I broke my silence to say to them, 'Sorry, ducks, I have nothing for you.' But they seemed content just to sit with me and be still.

I was to sing at a concert the day the retreat finished and had not practised all week. I wouldn't disturb anyone if I sang my song there in the bushland. But as I began, the ducks all got up and moved away. Humph, I thought, as they waddled off. Ducks as music critics. When I'd finished, they came back and gathered around me again, so we resumed our little Quaker meeting. I felt like a combination of Michael Leunig and St Francis of Assisi.

So of course there needed to be ducks on the Camino. And there were. Just that one family of them, that one day.

'Stay safe and be enriched'

I felt enriched from the first day. And safe. I do enjoy people-watching and had a whole day in Pamplona when I could do just that. I'm sure there are introverted, grumpy, morose Spaniards, but it I didn't see any. Not that day. The wide, open streets of old Pamplona are used mainly by pedestrians, but not just for getting somewhere else. People met in the streets, with much warmth and affection. They laughed a lot and seemed pleased to be there with each other. Especially with the children. The whole day I didn't hear one cross word directed at a child. We in Australia don't seem to like our children much. Not the way we treat them in public places. Supermarkets and restaurants and the like. In Pamplona they were treated with delight.

***

It was Sunday and raining as I entered the little village of Navarette. It felt like lunch time, so I found a small dry spot. Just one end of a concrete bench beside the main street. An over-hanging branch gave shelter from the rain. So I perched there, happily enough. Munching on my bread and cheese, with only the odd drop of water landing on me. But I must have looked pathetic. A man hurried out of a house across the road, carrying a glass and an open bottle of wine. He brought them across to me, pointing out the local region on the label. Maybe they were even his grapes.

It felt sacramental. His walk across the road an Offertory procession. I drank the wine with reverence as well as gratitude. Well, one glass, not the whole bottle.

***

All I'd read and heard about the meseta prepared me for an empty, featureless place. It was flat and hot and the villages were further apart. But, for someone who's met the challenge of playing I Spy with children while driving across the Hay Plain, the meseta wasn't featureless. I could have played I Spy all the way and not run out of words to use. Wildflowers grew beside the path, the fields were still a patchwork of colours and textures, and there were butterflies the colour of jacaranda blossoms.

***

On my second last day of the Camino, I lost my stick. Maybe I'd walk the last two days without one. I did that for half a day but it felt all wrong. My feet hurt without a stick to take some of the load and my pack was heavy and I just felt all out of kilter. I kept a lookout and tried a few possible substitutes and then, like Goldilocks, found one that was just right.

It seemed my stick had become a part of my walking. My new stick was straight and sturdy and served me for those last two days. It couldn't really take the place of my old one, but did the job in its own way. I considered throwing it into the sea but decided against that. It didn't seem right.

'Journey well; friends are with you'

I needed to hold on to that thought on the bus from Pamplona to Roncesvalles where my Camino was to begin. A busload of pilgrims, and I seemed to be the only English speaker. A moment of panic. Was this what my Camino would be like? Perhaps I'd walk the whole way without talking with another soul.

***

You can connect with people without talking. I became very fond of two young Polish sisters. One of them spoke only Polish, the other German as well, but no English. At least that's what I thought. Though one day she hurried past me to catch her sister who was far ahead. And said, 'Me sister is speed today.' We were always pleased to see each other, but one day they moved on. One of them held up her ten fingers three times the night before, so I guess that meant a thirty-kilometre day for them. Not for me, though.

***

The beetles didn't stop me. But they did make me think of Trish, a friend back home. As a child, Trish had a fight with her sister and decided to run away from home. She got as far as the lane behind her house. There her way was blocked by a menacing black beetle in the middle of the path. Whatever the difficulties at home, they were nothing compared to the threat of that beetle. So she gave up and went back. There were big black beetles on the Camino path. I didn't go back. But I thought of Trish each time. Fondly.

***

People came in and out of your life on the Camino. There were days when everyone I saw was someone I hadn't seen before. Then some days the 'oldies' would collect together in various combinations. As if in some pre-arranged rendezvous. Someone you thought long gone would suddenly be there, sitting outside a bar enjoying a morning coffee. Or they'd turn up at an albergue. We'd greet each other like long-lost friends, though even our greetings might be in different languages.

***

We spaced ourselves along the way. Spread ourselves out along the path. Many walking singly, in their own little Camino world, some in pairs, life partners or Camino liaisons of one kind or another, occasionally chatty little groups. Cyclists and faster walkers passed the others with a cheery Hola! or Buen Camino!

And then, in the villages, we'd clump together. We'd gather for morning coffee at a bar and at night in the albergues. A big extended family who assembled in various combinations. Then we'd go off again, to do our own thing. Then come together once more. There were some constants, but groupings formed and reformed. Randomly. At random times.

I'd lose contact with someone and suddenly there they'd be. When I walked into the albergue at Mansilla there was Bron, ex-punk rocker, artist, and real vegetarian, sitting in the reception area. She'd gone ahead but now had tendonitis in her foot and lost a day. You never knew who you'd meet at the next coffee bar or the next albergue or around the next bend. Always the chance you'd find someone you'd thought you'd lost.

'The secret spot'

My first night in Spain. Tucked away in my hotel room hearing the sounds of revelry outside. Knowing there would be no private sanctuary in my life for the next seven weeks. At least, no physical one. I felt I would miss that. I was right.

***

Just out of Ventosa, the path dipped down. A hollow between two small hills with dozens and dozens of little mounds spread out around the path. Made by pilgrims who had paused in their walking and piled stones. One on top of the other. There was something secret about that spot. I sat there in the secret and wondered what it was.

***

The churchyard at Ages was like that. Not the church itself. That was all gold and glitter. Like one more slice of chocolate gateau when what I really wanted was some plain, wholemeal bread. And the churchyard was it. A small enclosure with a lichen-clad stone wall, an iron gate, a couple of smallish trees. A bit overgrown with spindly grass and chamomile flowers. And beyond the wall, hills of green farmland. I sat for some time on a chunk of stone against the wall of the church and felt at peace with the world.

***

One morning on the meseta. I'd walked a few hours in the cool morning air, then started to descend to the little village of Hontanas. So different from the busy roads of Burgos. The quiet of the hills, the valley below. I sat in the stillness, to soak it up and carry away it with me.

'Breathe; be'

Welcome advice at the end of that first tiring day. To just sit, breathe, and be. That was enough.

***

Breathing and being were Camino lessons. Strange that we need lessons in them. Or that I did. Without them we'd die. Not exist. We have to do them. Why lessons? I'd lost them somehow. At least the awareness of them, if I ever had that. Being busy. Doing stuff. Getting tangled up in life. If I could just breathe and be, the rest would happen. Without me pushing and shoving.

Sometimes in Quaker meetings, I think of physics lessons. Early ones, about magnetism. That a magnetic material has domains, arranged randomly, pointing in all directions. If you stroke this material with a magnet, the domains line up, become ordered. I'd feel like that in meeting. Being stroked by some giant spiritual magnet. My disordered domains coming more aligned.

On the Camino it wasn't just the odd hour in meeting. I felt that stroking day after day. Soothing my inner disorder.

***

The albergue at Villamayor de Monjardin was run by a group of Dutch Christians. They invited us to a meditation session after dinner. I went along eagerly but, alas, no silence. Even when there wasn't talking, there was music. I like to sit in silence with others. Total silence. 'Mood' music didn't help.

***

I mostly walked by myself in a meditative kind of way. I counted my steps, and my breath followed the same pattern. A seven hundred and fifty kilometre walking meditation. Except for when I got distracted or the path was difficult or I came to a village or I walked with someone, or… Well, some of the seven hundred and fifty kilometres was a walking meditation.

'All truly good things are conceived by walking'

We sought different things from the Camino. Some were there for the walking and would not even call themselves pilgrims.

Some sought answers to life's problems. Like the young South African widow. She was certain she would meet someone or experience something that would point new direction for her life. Or the Spanish man who'd left his wife and four young children at home while he sought relief from his sadness and depression.

I was more at the stage of trying to find the question, let alone the answer.

***

I talked to a Danish man over dinner at Ages. His wife had walked the Camino two years before. She came back different. I asked in what way. She came back a much calmer person. And stayed that way. I too felt my knotty bits unravelling. Untangling as I walked the Camino.

***

Some were finding their jobs too stressful. The locksmith from England, the PA to the head of a multinational company in Germany, the director of a museum in Holland. All seeking ways to remove, or at least deal with, the stress of their lives.

Some had questions about career or study choices. Some were dealing with the loss of a loved one through death or separation. Some were coming to terms with, or testing, their body's limitations after illness or injury.

And we spoke of these things to each other. Over morning coffee at a village bar, at the evening meal, in the afternoon sitting around the albergue. The things we pondered as we walked. In our other lives, we would share these things with our closest friends. If that. Here we spoke of them with total strangers. But they were not total strangers. They were fellow peregrinos, all seeking to conceive of good things as they walked.

***

I met one man who had walked the Camino for the past ten years. He'd started from his home in Holland. Each year he'd spend his vacation walking a bit more. This year he expected to finish. His way was most unusual. He had both his car and a tiny motorcycle. Each day he drove his motorcycle to that day's finishing point. Ride back to his car at the end of the day, then drive off to some hotel, with good meals and accommodation. This was his vacation.

He said he wasn't a pilgrim, just someone who liked walking. Ten years of walking to Santiago. He was at a loss, though. What could he do next year?

'Look to the horizon'

I was walking the path one day, minding the mud and the stones and where to put my feet, when I chanced to look up. I was surrounded by fields of poppies. I stopped in wonder. I could have missed them. I was focusing so intently on walking the path, an important enough task, that I was quite unaware of what else was there, to be enjoyed and wondered at.

***

What I saw on the horizon was not always good. The climb up from Ages was steep. From there, on the horizon, beyond the green hills dotted with villages, was the city of Burgos. The air had been so fresh and clear and healthy. But hovering over Burgos was a very unhealthy-looking brown fog. I don't know whether it was rising up or going down, but either way it wasn't good news.

'You're supported by a host of unseen angels'

I started my pilgrimage at Roncesvalles on the Spanish side of the Pyrenees. Those who joined us from the French side had a terrible time. It had been cold. Really cold. With rain and wind and a thick fog, and mud calf-deep on the path. Many damaged their knees. Their Camino impaired. Perhaps their lives.

If it was unseen angels who gave me a little push in the direction of Roncesvalles, then I'd like to officially say Thank you. Shame about those others who didn't get pushed.

***

At times the supporting angels were far from unseen. Strangers helped me. So many times. Certainly when I asked, and often when I didn't. They just appeared and helped.

At Pamplona I was trying to buy my train ticket to return to Madrid from Santiago. We were struggling, the ticket seller and I. A young woman asked if I needed help. She sorted out the money side. My Spanish counting hadn't got to forty-three, let alone the bit after the decimal point. She said, Here's my phone number and here's my mother's. Ring if you need anything. She'd walked the Camino and understood.

I got lost a few times in Pamplona. I was new to Spain and it was all strange. I lost my hotel. You can't lose a hotel, but I did. Perhaps I'd passed this point a few times, with increasing anxiety, but a man there somehow knew I was looking for Calle San Nicolas, and came with me till I could see it.

***

I relished walking by myself. Just me and my soul making the journey. On the second day I was joined by a young Korean student, keen to work on her English. What's that? A slug. Say it again? Slug. S-lug. There were plenty of them so we had lots of practice. The walk to Santiago could become one long English lesson.

Then, at Uterga, another young Korean appeared and the two went off happily together. I said a little thank you to whatever unseen angel had brought them there. To the same place at the same time.

***

The guiding angels were often local residents, watching out lest we stray from the path and setting us aright. I was on the path to Logrono. It had merged with the road and then seemed to disappear. The path sometimes followed the road for a bit, but I could see no reassuring shells or arrows. A tractor came chugging along the road and the driver beeped his horn and pointed up the hill. Over there I could see a straggle of pilgrims winding their way up the path. Unnoticed by me, it had crossed to the other side of the road. Angels in Spain sometimes drive tractors.

***

Sometimes the angels were other pilgrims. One day I washed my other set of clothes and left them outside while I walked to the supermercado. The sky was darkening. Rapidly. I'd need to hurry to beat the rain. But it was faster and poured down while I was still shopping. Oh well, wet clothes to carry tomorrow. But, back at the albergue, someone had gathered up all the clothes and hung them on racks inside. Dry clothes after all.

***

Seamus and some others got lost one day. They had missed the markers and were starting to worry. Seamus said a little prayer and almost immediately a woman appeared, walking towards them. As 'she' approached, he realised that his angel was a heavily made-up transvestite, willing and able to show them the way.

Angels in pictures and statues look pretty androgenous. All the ones I've seen. A Spanish transvestite was a good version for the twenty-first century. Less scary than golden locks and wings and flowing robes would have been.

***

After my fall I spent a whole day in Castrojeriz. The albergue didn't open till three, so I bought a fresh supply of bread and cheese and found a shady spot to sit and eat. An oldish man walked past, paused, and looked at my lunch. 'Chorizo?' Not really my thing, but it seemed ungracious to say so. Sure enough, in a few minutes he was back with a packet. Several slices of something that looked like fatty, dark red, rindless bacon, strong-smelling. I did try, but I must confess I bundled most of it up with my lunch rubbish and hid it carefully in a bin. Angels mean well, but they don't always get it right.

***

I arrived at Trabedelo sick with a gastric bug, shivering with fever and not wanting to get out of bed. Then Leena came in. I met Leena, a Finnish woman, at Cacabelos, and thought, rather unkindly, typical school teacher. Knows everything and needs to tell everyone what she knows.

One of my Camino lessons is not to judge people too hastily. Leena had walked with a couple of Spanish men that day and the three of them took care of me. Brought me water, cooked plain boiled rice with garlic and found some chamomile tea. They must have reserved the room for me as well. I had it all to myself although it held two double bunks. Next morning they checked that I was well enough to leave. And wrote a note for the hospitalera saying that there was a woman upstairs who did not speak Spanish but who was sick and needed to stay another day.

Pilgrims did that for each other. For people they did not know and would probably never see again. Life can be that way.

***

I was walking along, following the yellow arrows, when suddenly, in the middle of the town of Melide, there were arrows pointing in two different directions. The one straight ahead to the church, and one to the left and the albergue. I didn't want either of those places. Which one led through the town to the Camino path?

I was standing pondering this question when I heard someone calling. Who and where? There, across the road in an upper window in the middle of this town, someone was calling to me, saying I should follow the left-hand arrow.

It was not only people in the street who gathered up lost peregrinos. Sometimes our guiding angels were tucked away in the upper stories of nearby buildings.

'May the blessings of Light be upon you'

The albergue at Trinidad de Arre had an air of calm grace and a wonderful walled garden. My guidebook said it had been a pilgrim hospital since the eleventh century. And the monk who greeted us (if such he was) may well have performed that duty for all those years. His silver hair shone like a halo. It matched his calm, benign manner as he meticulously selected us in order and recorded our particulars in the monastery register. There's probably a whole roomful somewhere. A record of all the pilgrims who have stayed at that place during those ten centuries.

***

The typical Spanish church, even in the smallest village, was incredibly ornate. The whole wall behind the altar shimmered with gold and was studded with statues and other decoration. There was often a statue of a dead Jesus reclining in a glass casket, bloodied wounds in his side, hands and feet, but with his head resting on a lacy pillow. Though I didn't much see the point in that for a dead person.

Not like a Quaker meeting house. They're usually plain to the point of austerity. I could sit in those ornate churches, though, and feel that sacred stillness I find in a meeting house. Especially if I closed my eyes.

***

After Burgos came the meseta, the high, flat, open grain-land. It was hot and almost treeless; quiet and empty with little to distract from the inner journey. I looked forward to the emptiness and wondered if the searing sun would serve as a searchlight for the soul. Or whether it would just be a bother.

***

At Leon the albergue was attached to a convent of Dominican nuns. Not that you'd know. They weren't visible. The only clue was the small discreet sign. No glitz. Not like some albergue signs that were big, bright and colourful.

There was a pilgrim blessing, held in the convent chapel between curfew and lights out. Then we saw them. Still wearing the habits that nuns in Australia used to wear. The service itself was standard stuff, prayers and psalms of a suitable kind. Spoken first in Spanish by an old nun, then in English by a young one. Always attributed. Mother says that…

At the end the nuns sang. A pure, clear sound, filling the old chapel. That was a blessing.

***

The albergue at O'Cebeiro was perched high on the top of a mountain, with layers of valleys and mountains all around. It was like scribbling on the Mona Lisa to hang clothes in front of it. But I did. I also sat and just looked. That felt more respectful. And all for three euros.

It was probably worth sleeping nose to nose with a stranger in the jammed-together bunks. I put my pillow at the other end of my bed. Nose to toes gave slightly more personal sleeping space than the usual arrangement did.

'May it be quality and quantity'

Bron was massaging her feet one day and saying what wonderful things they are. How grateful we should be to them. The big German walker said he hadn't realised there was a shortage of feet. But I think he was confusing quantity and quality.

If there's plenty of something, we can take it for granted. My mum admired nasturtiums. She said if they'd been rare they'd be appreciated. My brother Jim took a bunch to school one day to place in front of the Virgin's statue. The Brother threw them out, saying what an insult it was to offer those to Mary. They were too common to be of value. Does quantity diminish quality?

***

The cathedrals on the Camino were places of quality and quantity. No nasturtiums there. The first one, at Santo Domingo de la Calzada, was a massive structure, effectively turned into a museum. And guarded by the grumpiest lot of women you could imagine. None of them smiled. No warmth, no enthusiasm. A seeming reluctance to hand over a ticket. Perhaps they tired of tourists and pilgrims tramping through the cathedral. It didn't seem a place of worship.

So much to see there, though. Stone carvings and statues and paintings and carved wood choir stalls, soaring vaults, gold everywhere. And huge.

High above our heads was a light-filled recess with a glass front. In it, a pair of chooks. Both white. Apparently they get to spend a month there at a time, a reminder of the most famous story of Santo Domingo. So it's not all about Saint James.

The story goes that a couple and their teenage son stopped off at a local inn on their Camino journey. The innkeeper's daughter rather fancied the young man but he rebuffed her advances. A woman spurned…in this case planted a silver goblet in his rucksack and cried thief. The reluctant lover was duly hanged. But when the grieving parents came to collect his body, they found him very much alive. He said that Santo Domingo had miraculously saved him. But when they went to inform the corregidor, he didn't believe them. Their son was as alive as the cock and the hen he was about to eat. At which point the chooks started flapping their wings and crowing.

And there's part of the original gallows there in the cathedral as well, embedded in the wall just near the chooks. Which just goes to show it must be a true story.

***

I thought the cathedral at Santo Domingo was big and grand, but Burgos cathedral was bigger and grander. I didn't know it was possible to say Wow! so many times in the one building. Firstly for the building itself and all its fittings. Then for the objects it contained. There were so many and they were so magnificent that I was overwhelmed by them.

The most modest item was the plain marble slab marking the final resting place of El Cid and his spouse. They'd been interred in a couple of other places but ended up here. I didn't know much about him, except for an old Hollywood film I hadn't seen. I'd better check him out. There's sure to be something on the internet.

***

I visited the cathedral at Leon as well. Much of its wall space was made up of huge windows of stained glass. Rich colours and intricate designs. No lights inside. Perhaps they'd detract from the windows' splendour. But it gave the place a drab, dingy feel. And it was cold.

By that stage I'd done cathedrals. And churches generally. I didn't want to see another bleeding Jesus. Or a sorrowful Madonna. Or San Sebastion standing there with all those arrows sticking out of him, blood trickling down from every wound. Spanish churches are full of such images. That and glittering gold. Where's the joy in that?

'Travel well, dear friend'

The Camino path is across the top of Spain from east to west. I started each morning at first light and walked until the middle of the day. The sun as I started was low on the horizon. By the time I stopped, it was high in the sky. Each day, each step I took was a step into my own ever-shortening shadow.

***

Leena said you could tell the pilgrims. In the daytime by their backpacks and at night by their hobble. That's the walking pilgrims. The cycling ones were different. They zoomed past on their bikes – no backpacks – often calling out a greeting as they went. At night they moved differently too. Their feet hadn't walked all day and so they came clomping in heavily in their cycling shoes. Quite unlike the walkers' careful shuffle.

They often travelled in groups and, as they rode, needed to shout to be heard by each other. And they forgot that they didn't need to do that once they'd dismounted. Their sense of personal space included their bicycles. Unlike the walkers whose sense of self included body (especially feet and legs), backpack and stick. The cyclists' selves took up bike-sized space in the albergues as well as on the road.

The walkers sometimes read their guidebooks at night and made tentative plans for tomorrow. Their way was marked by arrows and shells and they only needed to look out for those along the way. But the cyclists measured each day's journey in hundreds rather than tens of kilometres. They needed to know where they were going. So they'd pore over real maps, making serious plans for tomorrow. They were always the first to leave and the last to arrive. No slow starts or early afternoons for them. Peregrinos like us. But different.

And then there were the classy walkers. Those who stayed at mysterious places and who strolled along with designer clothes and their tiny backpacks. Carrying goodness knows what, as a van came along bringing their no doubt gourmet snacks and refreshments to pre-determined spots. They were peregrinos too, though they didn't have the sweaty, scruffy, laden look of the regular walkers.

***

As I approached the tiny village of Moratinos, there was something funny about the hill. It looked like dog kennels stuck in the hillside. Small arched openings at any rate. As I came closer they got bigger. Too big for dogs. They were doorways. With doors. There were chimneys sticking out too, one with a television antenna. They must be houses. Little hobbit houses burrowing into the hillside. I went as close as seemed decent. I wanted to go closer, but these were, after all, people's homes and I was just a pilgrim passing by.

'Way will open'

It wasn't so much the way that opened at Mansilla but, rather, the albergue. Usually there was a curfew at ten o'clock or so. Doors locked, lights out. But that night Spain was playing Germany in the European football finals and not even the gates of the albergue could prevail against that. The curfew was extended to midnight. And Spain won. A few hoarse throats and sore heads the next day. But my earplugs did their job. Beyond the first few chorus roars from the bar next door, I was oblivious to the whole thing.

***

Sometimes I planned to do one thing and something else happened instead. My careful plans fell apart and an unexpected path opened. Sometimes quite literally. There were two routes from Triacastela to Sarria. One was considerably shorter, following the road rather than the wooded hills. I'd lost a bit of time one way and another, so decided on this one. Not so beautiful, but shorter, quicker, flatter.

So I turned right rather than left and headed off, alert for the first landmark. It didn't appear. After a few kilometres I realised I was on the wooded way. How did that happen? I'm sure I started in the shorter direction.

The hill path, the one I was on, was through lush, damp greenery. Trees, moss, ferns, leaves on the path. It reminded me of Queensland rainforest. I used to live there and I pine for it sometimes, from the harsh dryness of South Australia where I live now. The hill walk juiced my soul. It was worth the extra six kilometres.

***

The journey from Palas de Ru to Melide wasn't a long enough walk for one day, but I didn't want to go an extra eleven kilometres to get to Ribadiso. My guidebook said that's where I'd find the next albergue. There was a village the right distance in between, but with no accommodation listed. Please God, may someone have opened one there.

No posters or signs along the way as there usually were with a new albergue, so not much hope. I stopped in a shady spot for a quick lunch. I'd walked twelve kilometres, over a steep mountain, when I was really sick. Surely I can walk another five and a half kilometres when I'm only hot and tired.

And there it was. A little hand-painted sign, 'Albergue'. My leap (or rather trudge) of faith had paid off. Above a tiny bar just down the hill from the Camino path. A room with only two bunk beds in it, and a bathroom with a real bath. Perfecto!

'Kerry, all the best'

Most of the towns and villages seemed poor, quaint in a down-at-heel kind of way. They probably welcomed the trickle of euros the passing pilgrims left. Molinaseca was not like that. It was on a river, down from the mountains. An old stone bridge over the river and parks alongside. Prosperous-looking buildings and prosperous-looking people. Tourists too probably. One of the best places. I felt too shabby to go into the trendy-looking shops and bars, even if I changed into my clean clothes.

***

Sometimes it's hard to know what 'the best' is. For two successive nights I stayed in municipal albergues in O'Cebeiro and Triacastela. The settings were the best, but inside was crowded and noisy. My days were filled with silence. The noise there assaulted my senses.

This was the last section of the Camino. There would be more and more groups of young people, holidaying for a couple of weeks on the Camino. If they walked one hundred kilometres they could get the certificate, the compestela, to show for it. And good luck to them. But sharing my evening, and early morning, space with their boisterous good humour was a challenge I didn't relish.

They were likely to stay at the cheap, municipal albergues which didn't need my patronage any longer. I'd set aside my socialist principles and seek out the more upmarket private albergues. For the last few days.

So at Sarria, I found myself at a private albergue high on a hill in the historic old area of town. Sitting alone on the rooftop terrace with a view of town and country and just fifty metres away from the clock tower of the big old church. Fortunately the clock was not working.

Though I'd learned to sleep through a lot over the previous five weeks. I would hardly have noticed the clanging of eight old iron bells every quarter hour.

***

Santa Irene was the last stop before Santiago and I headed straight for the 'privado' albergue. Plenty of space, soft lighting, gracious décor, gracious hospitalera. Best of all, because I was the first to arrive 'solo', I had a single bed off by itself in a little alcove where the ceiling was too low for a double bunk. This was the most expensive albergue I stayed in and it was only twelve euros.

I'm glad I experienced the budget, three-euro albergues. But they did bad things for my soul. You probably need to be young and with a group of extrovert friends to enjoy them.

'Kia ora, kia kaha'

This Maori blessing translates as 'Be well, be strong' and I needed that on my biggest adventure.

It was my second day on the meseta. I'd started to walk in the cool of the early morning and by midday was just about at Castrojeriz. I'd intended to stop there. Someone was about to overtake me and I turned to say Hola to Seamus, the Irishman, when somehow my feet tangled with each other and down I went.

With a pack on your back, the ground comes up pretty fast and my forehead crashed into the gravel before I could do anything to save myself. I could feel the blood on my face and see it spattered on the lenses of my glasses. I didn't feel great. But Seamus and a few others tended my wound. They flagged down a passing motorist who drove me and Seamus to the albergue. But no doctor in the village on Sunday. The albergue would not open for another three hours so we sat in the porch and wondered what to do. I needed some attention but I'd no idea how much. Seamus was sure it needed stitching. Four or five local lads gathered. We provided some excitement on a dull Sunday afternoon.

Seamus spoke slightly more Spanish than I and the boys spoke even less English. A phone was produced and passed from one to the other to fill in various bits of the story. An ambulance was on its way.

I hate fuss, but I was now at the centre of an ever bigger and more public drama. The ambulance came quietly. No sirens or flashing lights. Fortunately. And, no, they wouldn't take me to the hospital in Burgos, but to a medical centre... somewhere else. And, no, Seamus couldn't come too, only the patient.

We drove for what I estimated to be between fifteen and thirty minutes. My watch had stopped that morning so I had no way of knowing just how long it was. The ambulance attendants spoke no

English. Neither did those who attended me at the medical centre. They cleaned the wound and taped it together. None too gently. Perhaps they thought it was my own silly fault; only mad dogs and peregrina Ingles would walk in weather like this. Maybe it was Fancy making all this fuss over a little cut like that. There was no way of knowing. Or perhaps it was just the way they were.

Then I was told, in effect, you can go now. Great. Go where? I asked where I was, 'Donde es?' and was told something that to my English language ears sounded very like blah blah blah blah blah. The ambulance people said they couldn't take me back to Castrojeriz. Someone asked, 'Telefono?' but who could I phone? I didn't want any more adventure, I just wanted to rest awhile, so I asked, 'Hostal?' One of the ambulance people wrote Hostal Concha on a piece of paper and that was it. Off you go.

There are still times in my life when all I want to do is sit down on the ground and howl, 'I want my mummy.' This was one of those times. There I was in a very drab-looking town, I didn't know where it was or what it was called, somewhere in the north of Spain. Turned out it was Melgar de Fernamental. I was hot and sweaty. My head hurt and I must have looked a sight.

The daggy clothes, backpack and walking stick identify you as a peregrina on the Camino. Somewhere else, I probably just looked like an ageing hobo, especially with my blood-spattered shirt and my injured head. This was not Camino country and it wasn't tourist territory either. I was probably the first non-Spanish person to visit the town in living memory. So there I was, alone in the street, holding my little scrap of paper containing the words Hostal Concha. It's the sort of thing nightmares are made of. But even as I thought that, I also thought, Wait till I tell them back home about this little episode.

I was starting to feel a little teary and somewhat sorry for myself, but then I said, C'mon, Kez, this is an adventure. Everyone has their own Camino and this is yours. It's only a problem to be solved. You can do that.

I set off down the street and came to a bookshop that was open and asked for directions. There was even a young woman who spoke some English. She was able to point me to Hostal Concha. She asked if I'd like her to come with me, but I was beginning to feel brave again so said, No thanks, I'll be fine.

I found Hostal Concha and told my story as best I could. I probably didn't look the most desirable of customers, but they gave me a room. Tucked away in a corner upstairs.

What to do next? A warm shower, like a good sleep, does wonders for any situation. Somewhat revived, and a lot cleaner, I took my list of Camino places to ask the man at the desk. Was there a bus to any of them? None to any of the intermediate places. One to big and bustling Burgos (two days back) and one to Leon (seven days ahead). 'Hoy? Today?' he asked. Was that a hopeful question? I wasn't adding to the tone of their clientele and they sure weren't in Good Samaritan mode.

Maybe I could go back to Burgos and see if I could find a bus from there to get me back on track again. Or maybe I could walk to Castrojeriz if I had a map. Or even get a taxi, if there was such a thing in Melgar de Fernamental. If it wasn't going to cost the earth. One thing for sure. I just wanted to spend the day (and night) quietly in Melgar de Fernamental. Worry about it all mañana.

Besides, when I went back, the bookshop had closed. So I couldn't find a map there to see where I was in relation to the Camino or to anything else.

So, back to the hostal. There were now people in the dining room who looked at me curiously as I walked through. I tried not to slink and walked tall with as much dignity as I could scrape together. Under the circumstances, it wasn't a lot. I had promised myself at least one night in somewhere other than the albergues, but this wasn't quite what I'd had in mind.

And to top it all off, they locked me in. Maybe they'd forgotten I was there or whoever locked up didn't know. I went downstairs about eight to find some dinner, but the door to the dining room was locked and the room in darkness. Maybe the restaurant closed Sunday nights. Through there was the only way I knew to get out. So I went back up to my room and perched on my bed to eat the last of my bread and cheese. Like the little hostal mouse nibbling quietly away in the corner.

In the morning I went down to reception. There was just a little old lady who didn't seem to understand when I asked about a taxi.

Instead, she led me quickly out the back door, pointing out, 'Cafeteria enfrente (opposite).' No breakfast in the dining room for the likes of me. So I had a coffee and a custard pastry, being stared at all the while by the all-male clientele. The proprietor wished me Buen Camino as I left, so the odd pilgrim must stray in that direction.

But that was the question. What direction? I headed back to the bookshop. It was open this time so I asked if they had a map. They had plenty, mostly of the whole of Spain. How far, and in what direction was the village Castrojeriz? About seventeen kilometres and (we were outside now) up that road and then turn right.

By this time, another little crowd had gathered. At least I was providing some entertainment for the locals. I could walk back to the Camino, but it was now after nine and getting hotter and I still wasn't feeling great. Castrojeriz? said one chap (all in Spanish but I got the gist). I'll take you there. And so he did, chatting all the way.

He spoke no English, but that didn't deter him. I picked up a few odd bits. His son was (or had been) in England. Or maybe spoke English. The road was busy and the trucks took up too much room. Castrojeriz had once been home to... Muslims? I suggested (I knew this had been Moor country). No, not Muslims. Jews? Yes, that's it, Jews. And a great deal more besides. And I nodded and smiled a lot. The universal response of non-comprehension.

But I was very grateful to yet another Spanish angel who had guided me back to the Camino.

I'd managed difficult paths. Steep, rocky, muddy, slippery. Yet, I fell while walking along level ground. Perhaps they are the dangerous bits. The seemingly uneventful times when there are no obvious challenges. We take it all for granted and slip into neutral. Or slip another way.

***

Mostly I could see other pilgrims visible before and behind me, but sometimes I felt as though I was the only one on the Camino; no one else in sight. Whichever way, I felt safe, though there was the odd moment when I'd rather not have been alone.

On one such day, a couple of hounds came bounding towards me, ears flapping, tongues lolling. And then a man with a stick, occasionally beating the bushes by the side of the path. I gave the usual Hola! Unlike everyone else I met on the way, he just scowled at me. Silently. As we were about to pass, he turned and began walking in my direction, about twenty paces ahead. It was disconcerting.

But then, soon enough, he turned down a side path, the dogs leaping about him as he went.

I suppose he was trying to flush some quarry from the bushes, though I've no idea what. He did me no harm, nor did his dogs, but I was pleased to see him go. The only moment of unease on the whole Camino.

'Go, Kez; all will be well'

I came back convinced of that. The underlying wellness of it all. There are wrongs and there are evils, but there is also something good about people and about the world.

I don't really know how, or if, my Camino experience has changed me. I think we are changed by every experience. With one as profound as this, I must surely have changed. Significantly. I find it hard to stand back and look at the before and after Kerrys and spot the differences. But there are some things I learned.

I met people from such different backgrounds and with such different personalities and motivations. But with a common humanity. We took time, had time, to really listen to each other's stories, to (as the Quaker saying goes) know one another in the things that are eternal. There is probably no greater gift we humans can give to each other. We were willing to risk sharing those deep and vulnerable things about ourselves. And felt safe doing so.

I felt moved by the beauty I encountered. The beauty of the earth and of human things. I carry that awe and wonder within me.

I felt great satisfaction in achieving a difficult goal. And of persevering through adversity. I was helped when I needed it and offered help to others when that seemed right. But I managed a great deal on my own and I am proud of that. I know I've done a difficult and challenging thing, and so do my children and my grandchildren. That's now become a benchmark for all life's challenges. When faced with an onerous task, a difficult person, an insoluble problem, I say, I walked across Spain. I can do that.

Living for that time with so little, I appreciate anything more. The joy of a freshly made bed, the luxury of personal space, the indulgence of more than two sets of clothes. I am grateful for those things. They enrich my life.

I still carry with me the stillness of all that silent walking. I hold on to it. The silent space in my life. I have no television, almost no radio. I don't even want music in my daily life. That all feels too intrusive.

I have even less of a sense of a deity 'out there' than before I went. My awe and reverence and gratitude is not directed towards an external being. Whatever wisdom I seek must come from that deep stillness within myself and within others. The silent and uncluttered knowing that is the ground and depth of our being.

I gained not so much a greater clarity about life as a sense of conundrum. That everything both matters intensely and matters not at all. I can't explain that, but there it is. I feel a pervasive sense of personal peace and a desire to live life more slowly, to savour it more. And I relish the spirit of adventure that led me to do this thing.

I delight too in the love and affection of my family and friends. I'm more aware of that and grateful for it. I was nurtured and sustained by the messages I carried on my stick. Almost all the way across the Camino. And of the care and devotion those messages stood for.

People may look at me now and see a little (I don't yet say old) white-haired lady. I look quite ordinary.

They don't know. But I know.

I walked the Camino.

www.ingramcontent.com/pod-product-compliance
Lightning Source LLC
Chambersburg PA
CBHW030912080526
44589CB00010B/275